My State

HAWAII

By Christina Earley

TABLE OF CONTENTS

A Crabtree Seedlings Book

Crabtree Publishing

crabtreebooks.com

School-to-Home Support for Caregivers and Teachers

This book helps children grow by letting them practice reading. Here are a few guiding questions to help the reader build his or her comprehension skills. Possible answers appear in red.

Before Reading:

- What do I know about Hawaii?
    - *I know that Hawaii is a state.*
    - *I know that Hawaii has beaches.*

- What do I want to learn about Hawaii?
    - *I want to learn which famous people were born in Hawaii.*
    - *I want to learn what the state flag looks like.*

During Reading:

- What have I learned so far?
    - *I have learned that Honolulu is the state capital of Hawaii.*
    - *I have learned that sometimes it snows on Mauna Kea, Mauna Loa, and Haleakala.*
- I wonder why...
    - *I wonder why the state flower is the yellow hibiscus.*
    - *I wonder why they grow so many pineapples in Hawaii.*

After Reading:

- What did I learn about Hawaii?
    - *I have learned that the only coconut farm in Hawaii is in Lahaina.*
    - *I have learned that the state animal is the Hawaiian monk seal.*

- Read the book again and look for the glossary words.
    - *I see the word **capital** on page 6, and the word **windsurfing** on page 17. The other glossary words are found on pages 22 and 23.*

HAWAII
Hi! My name is Keoni.
Welcome to Hawaii!

I live in Lahaina. My city is on the island of Maui.

Lahaina has the only coconut farm in Hawaii.

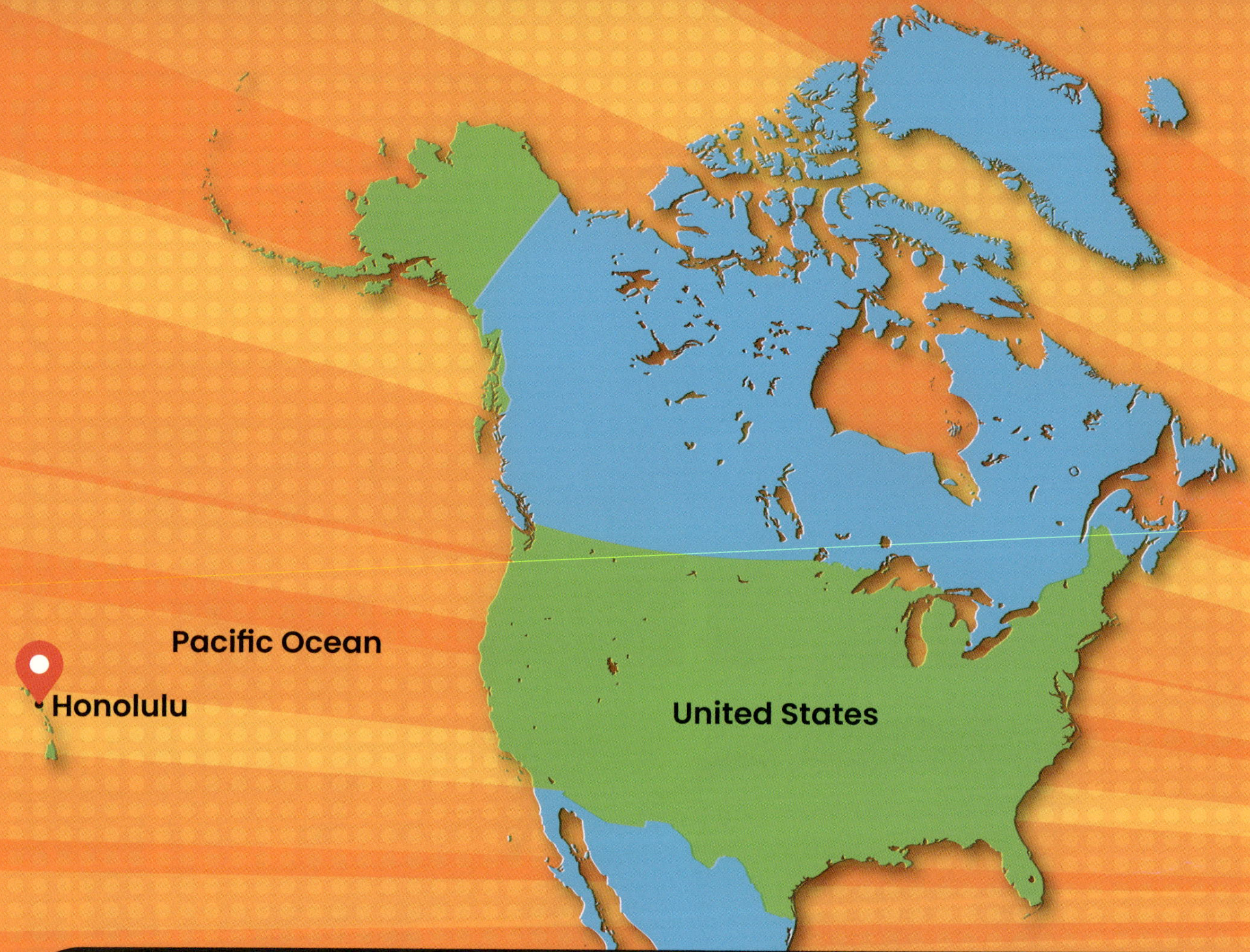

Hawaii is made up of a group of islands in the Pacific Ocean. The **capital** is Honolulu.

Fun Fact: Honolulu is the largest city in Hawaii.

The state animal is the Hawaiian monk seal.

The yellow hibiscus is the state flower.

We grow a lot of pineapples. Some of them are used to make my favorite dessert, pineapple upside-down cake.

Fun Fact: Hawaii **produces** more than 400 million pineapples a year.

My state flag has red, white, and blue stripes.

The United Kingdom's Union Jack flag is in the corner.

The islands of Hawaii were formed by **volcanoes**. Kilauea and Mauna Loa are volcanoes that still **erupt**.

Fun Fact: Sometimes it snows on the volcanoes Mauna Kea, Mauna Loa, and Haleakala.

My family and I like to go for drives on the Hana Highway. The curves and bridges make the drive an adventure!

We watch people **windsurfing** at Ho'okipa Lookout.

Singer Bruno Mars was born in Hawaii. Surfer Bethany Hamilton was also born in Hawaii.

Fun Fact: President Barack Obama was born in Honolulu, Hawaii.

I like to learn about the history of **Polynesia** at the Polynesian Cultural Center.

I enjoy exploring Waimea Canyon.

Glossary

capital (cap-ih-tuhl): The city or town where the government of a country, state, or province is located

erupt (ih-rupt): To explode

Polynesia (pol-uh-nee-zhuh): Islands of the central and southern Pacific Ocean, including Hawaii

produces (pruh-doos-es): Makes or grows something for sale or use

volcano (vol-kay-noh): A mountain with an opening that sometimes sends out an explosion of lava, rocks, and ash

windsurfing (wind-ser-fing): Riding along the surface of the water while standing on a long board that has a sail attached to it

Index

About the Author

Christina Earley lives in sunny South Florida with her husband and son. She enjoys traveling around the United States and learning about different historical places. Her hobbies include hiking, yoga, and baking.

Written by: Christina Earley
Designed and Illustrated by: Bobbie Houser
Series Development: James Earley
Proofreader: Melissa Boyce
Educational Consultant: Marie Lemke M.Ed.

Photographs:
Alamy: WENN: p. 18 left
Shutterstock: Chris Howey: cover; Ryan Tishken: p. 3; EQRoy: p. 4; michel arnault: p. 5; pingebat: p. 6, 22; Izabela23: p. 7; Lorraine Logan: p. 8; Khanchit Kamboobpha: p. 9; ShishkaBob: p. 10-11; Kotcha K: p. 11, 23; Millenius: p. 12; lazyllama: p. 13; Gambarini Gianandrea: p. 14-15, 22; LUC KOHNEN: p. 15, 23; Kelly Headrick: p. 16; K.L. Kohn: p. 17, 23; Featureflash Photo Agency: p. 18 right; Boykov: p. 20, 22; Martin M303: p. 21
White House: p. 19

Crabtree Publishing

crabtreebooks.com 800-387-7650

Printed in the U.S.A./012023/CG20220815

Published in Canada
Crabtree Publishing
616 Welland Avenue
St. Catharines, Ontario
L2M 5V6

Published in the United States
Crabtree Publishing
347 Fifth Avenue
Suite 1402-145
New York, New York, 10016

Library and Archives Canada Cataloguing in Publication
Available at Library and Archives Canada

Library of Congress Cataloging-in-Publication Data
Available at the Library of Congress

Hardcover: 978-1-0398-0245-2
Paperback: 978-1-0398-0255-1
Ebook (pdf): 978-1-0398-0275-9
Epub: 978-1-0398-0265-0

NCTE Editorial Board

Can We Talk?

Can We Talk?

Encouraging Conversation in High School Classrooms

Susanne Rubenstein

NCTE

National Council of Teachers of English
340 N. Neil St., Suite #104, Champaign, Illinois 61820
www.ncte.org

Staff Editor: Cynthia Gomez
Manuscript Editor: Bonny Graham
Interior Design: Jenny Jensen Greenleaf
Cover Design: Christina DeYoung
Cover Image: Marvin Young

Print ISBN: 978-0-8141-0432-3; ebook ISBN: 978-0-8141-0434-7

It is the policy of NCTE in its journals and other publications to provide a forum for the open discussion of ideas concerning the content and the teaching of English and the language arts. Publicity accorded to any particular point of view does not imply endorsement by the Executive Committee, the Board of Directors, or the membership at large, except in announcements of policy, where such endorsement is clearly specified.

NCTE provides equal employment opportunity to all staff members and applicants for employment without regard to race, color, religion, sex, national origin, age, physical, mental or perceived handicap/disability, sexual orientation including gender identity or expression, ancestry, genetic information, marital status, military status, unfavorable discharge from military service, pregnancy, citizenship status, personal appearance, matriculation or political affiliation, or any other protected status under applicable federal, state, and local laws.

Every effort has been made to provide current URLs and email addresses, but, because of the rapidly changing nature of the web, some sites and addresses may no longer be accessible.

Library of Congress Control Number: 2022946

Ah, good conversation—there's nothing like it, is there?
The air of ideas is the only air worth breathing.
—Edith Wharton

Contents

Acknowledgments

This book is a thank you to every student who was brave enough to raise a hand, share a thought, and contribute to the conversation in our classroom. And it is an apology to every student who needed more of my encouragement to find the courage to speak.

To those whose conversation sustained me through the lonely months of the pandemic, thank you. Your voices, whether from across the kitchen table, the country road I live on, or the telephone line, took me out of myself and into another world, as all good conversation should do. Those days reminded me just how much we all need the connection and comfort of conversation, and how lucky we are when together we find those moments when we can talk.

Introduction

Give me the gift of a listening heart.

—King Solomon

When I begin a book, the introduction is as much for me as for my readers. I always feel I need to write the introduction first in order to rethink for myself the ideas I want to talk about. Putting those ideas in words on a page confirms for me why I am writing the book. The introduction takes me to the heart of what I am doing.

This time I struggled to write this opening. The words didn't come, and so I jumped into the chapters, all the while wondering why I couldn't find that beginning and if maybe what I thought I had to say didn't matter much after all. I felt almost afraid that what I wanted to say wouldn't resonate with teachers in the twenty-first century. And then COVID-19 hit and the world turned upside down. In the turmoil of the ensuing days, the days I'm living through now as I write this introduction, my uncertainty has disappeared. I know for sure why this book matters, why conversation matters, and why we *must* talk with one another.

In the first week of turmoil, as schools shut down, as grocery store shelves emptied, as we all tried to find a way to navigate the new normal, I had long telephone conversations with three of the people I care most for in the world. Interestingly enough, I couldn't have said when I had last actually had a long conversation with any of these people, either in person or over the phone. The first of the three was my niece, whom I had last seen weeks before in the happy chaos of a family celebration. The second was a colleague and good friend whom I often see only at department meetings, as her classroom is two floors below mine, our teaching schedules and free periods rarely jibe, and our lives are eternally busy. The third was my best friend, whom I last saw for a goodbye hug two months earlier as she was about to leave for a teaching position across the world. So it's not that I had been entirely out of contact with these people. We had communicated in all the ways technology and time seemed to allow, but *we had not spoken in any depth*. Quick exchanges, cheery emails, a card in the mail, but conversation? No. Yet in the early days of the COVID-19 crisis, we spoke, and we talked in a way that I remember talking before technology took hold of us. Our telephone conversations were long and rambling, and we moved from one topic to another as the spirit moved us. At one point, my niece said hesitatingly, "I wasn't even going to bring this up, but . . . ," and began to talk about a piece of her life that she suddenly felt she wanted to share, maybe because it felt right, maybe because the leisurely conversation welcomed it, maybe because I was there listening, murmuring encouragingly, asking questions to clarify, and hearing more than her words through the timbre of her voice. None of the three conversations was planned; there was no agenda, no list of points to cover, no expected time constraints. All three of the conversations involved hearty shared laughter, despite the conditions we were all facing, and the laughter buoyed us and kept us talking. And all three of the conversations ended with a promise to talk again soon, very soon. In fact, one closed with the words, "Can we talk again this week?"

After two weeks of school shutdowns, my colleagues and I were suddenly thrust into a world of remote learning. Difficult at best, even harder for someone like me who is not a fan of online learning, I found myself scrambling to adjust to the technological demands. For me, finding a way to communicate, both efficiently and personally, with my 140-plus students seemed daunting, to say the least, and despite all the emails and directives from those in charge, I was fumbling and frustrated and felt doomed. After a flurry of emails that simply confused me more, I sent an administrator one more email, asking if I might call him. He was gracious and helpful and immediately sent his phone number. I called, he answered, and within minutes, after a series of clear and pleasant exchanges, my immediate problems were solved and I breathed easier. And all I could think was how glad I was that I had typed the words *"Can we talk?"*

Finally, an invitation came from another dear friend, also quite far away, suggesting an online Zoom gathering where eight old friends would connect, commiserate, and hopefully cheer one another on as the dark days continued. But after having spent weeks in more online faculty and department meetings than I cared to count, I just couldn't quite rally to meet on a screen for fun. The awkward, staccato rhythm of an online meeting felt little like human connection, but rather an activity that only emphasized the abnormality of the times. So I declined with what I hoped was a polite email, but I'm sure my words came across as brusque at best, more likely cranky, and so this very good friend reached out and phoned me. We talked, our conversation bounding back and forth as each of us tried to explain our positions on this way of connecting. I heard myself saying, "No, no, I meant . . . ," "But are you saying . . .?," and the like, clarifying my words as she did the same. When we ended the phone call, we both better understood the other's feelings. And then the next morning an email came in which my friend wrote, "I'm really glad we had the conversation about how electronic communication feels to you. . . . Once again it has made me think, 'Oh, . . . of course . . . I never thought about it that way. . . .' As we make our way through this extraordinary new time, I feel like that happens to me over and over again, and I want to keep paying close attention to everything I learn." I read her words and thought, so can we talk again soon?

These three anecdotes are meant to illustrate the power of conversation. Though most sources define *conversation* simply as two or more people talking together, I much prefer Robert Frost's reflection on conversation: "I was under twenty when I deliberately put it to myself one night after good conversation that there are moments when we actually touch in talk what the best writing can only come near" (qtd. in Jost 397). Something happens in conversation that goes beyond a simple exchange of words. Conversation is human connection with an element of risk. When we open our mouths to speak, we don't always know what we are about to say, and we can't take our words back. We put ourselves in a vulnerable position when we engage in conversation, and we grow in an understanding of ourselves and others as a result. Though sometimes verbal communication can be awkward or tedious or even painful, often it is, as Anne Morrow Lindbergh describes, "as stimulating as black coffee and just as hard to sleep after" (102). Those are the conversations that make us feel alive—and truly connected. Those are the moments we can experience *if* we make the time to talk and allow ourselves to speak the truth.

There is nothing normal about these days of COVID-19, and even the most optimistic among us are hard pressed to find any sort of silver lining in all the tragedy we have seen. But here is something I suspect most of us will take away from the long months and now years of the pandemic. The virus and the new way of life it demands have reminded us of our humanity and of what we need to survive as human beings, and that is empathy, compassion, and connection. Certainly, social media has helped with all three (those of us of a certain age can't help but wonder how different this experience might be were it happening in the days before the internet), but my experiences with people close to me have highlighted, emphasized, and ultimately convinced me that we absolutely need conversation if we are to thrive. In conversation, words are spoken, heard, and responded to without the "benefit" of a delay or a delete. Conversation is freeform and often freewheeling. It lacks the safety net of written communication, with time to process an idea, to seek additional input, to review and revise a response, or to ignore someone's words entirely. Conversation is risky, and for that very reason it exposes us as individuals and reveals our true selves. For the very same reason, it is wonderful and illuminating and intensely human.

With each month of the stay-at-home order, conversation becomes even more important. The phone rings and I feel my spirits lift, or I am outside on my daily constitutional and someone headed the other way, masked like me, pauses and, across the country road I live on, we call to each other in conversation. These opportunities for spoken words, spontaneous and sincere, hearten me, and remind me, in a way that no email or text does, that I am not alone.

So perhaps, especially after having endured months of social isolation, we'd all agree on the importance of conversation in the social sphere. Yet, curiously, I'm not so sure we all recognize that it is equally important in the classrooms where we teach. In classrooms packed with students and stuffed with required curriculum, with bells ringing and tests looming, it's easy to regard conversation as a luxury, as a frill, maybe even as an outmoded teaching strategy. I believe that is a loss and perhaps even an assault to our humanity. I hope this book will convince other teachers of that. If we as human beings learn best when learning involves human connection, we must embrace and encourage the power of conversation.

Although this book is about conversation in the classroom and ways that we can promote an authentic exchange of ideas among our students, I'd like to add here that, as educators, we also need to make more time for conversation among ourselves. We need meetings that do more than disseminate information. We need professional development that goes beyond the lecture of a supposed expert. We need time in the school day to sit down and talk to one another about the challenges we are facing and the solutions we are finding. We need to connect to one another as people, not only as pieces of data in an administrator's report.

Even now, as I end this introduction, I'm wishing that I could sit in a room with those teachers who are reading these pages. I wish that instead of me "speaking" and readers just "listening," we could have a conversation where our words would fly back and forth in all their unscripted glory, and we could hear one another's ideas, opinions, and laughter. Simply, I wish I could say to all of you, "Can we talk?"—and that in that conversation, we would find true connection.

It is quite honestly difficult to write a book like this in a time that is so out of time. It is even harder, many months later, to edit it and to smoothly straddle that line between what was and what is. When I first wrote this introduction, I ended with this paragraph:

> As September nears, so too does the idea of continued remote learning. It almost feels a bit delusional to be touting ideas for classroom conversation when classroom doors are locked or students sit in semi-isolation. But I remind myself that there will come a time when we do all return to our classrooms, and I suspect there will be extraordinary joy in that coming together. Perhaps all these months of separation will have made us thirsty for conversation, and perhaps we, both teachers and students, will have a newfound appreciation for the sound of human voices around us. Perhaps we won't have to ask, "Can we talk?" Perhaps we will simply rejoice in the fact that we finally can.

I think maybe I was a little optimistic. Now, more than one September later and finally back in our classrooms, I know we all do feel this joy. We are grateful to be together, teachers and students alike, and we're poised to share our thoughts, our stories, our selves. *Finally*, we think, we can talk. But can we? The permission to meet face to face and to engage in real conversation is only part of it. For our students, there is also the question of ability, and it seems the long months of isolation have only exacerbated the struggle many of them face when it comes to spoken communication. They are literally at a loss for words at a time when they desperately need to find true human connection. So though the question is still "Can we talk?," I believe the answer now is "We must talk." As teachers, we have to make conversation happen.

I

Understanding the Problem

It is the encounters with people that make life worth living.
—*Guy de Maupassant*

This book was born out of a conversation, one carried on in a Baltimore restaurant over soft-shell crab sandwiches and iced tea. The two of us were catching up, and at some point, the conversation turned, as it inevitably does when two people involved in education meet, to "kids today." We shared stories of children and students, and suddenly I found myself announcing, "Kids today don't know how to talk." It wasn't the first time I'd thought that, but I think it was the first time I'd said it aloud, and somehow the vehemence of that statement combined with the questions the two of us tossed back and forth—"Is it because of technology?" "What sort of opportunities do they have to talk?" "Do they even *want* to talk?"—became the idea for a book—even before the check arrived.

There is no question in my mind that this book would not have been written without that conversation. No number of emails or texts would have allowed the space and spontaneity of that conversation, and though I might still be grumbling to myself that kids today don't know how to talk, I wouldn't have had an audience for my thoughts, and I probably wouldn't have explored those thoughts any further—or the delete key would have allowed me to reconsider. The philosopher John Armstrong writes, "[Conversation] is an unrehearsed intellectual adventure." I was lucky that day to experience such an adventure with someone who listened and spoke and challenged and questioned—and made me feel free to do the same. I have come to believe that students today rarely have such an experience, and the absence of this sort of engagement leaves them something close to speechless.

And that is the problem. They seem unable to talk. Even students themselves are aware of it. They struggle to talk, in class and out, to adults, to their families, even to their friends. They sit alone in their bedrooms or basements, they hide behind screens, they panic when a situation requires conversation. They struggle to find words to express what they are feeling, and when the words do come, they hold them back, scared to say what they're thinking. They are twenty-first-century kids, practically born with a smartphone in their hands into a world where change is the only constant. And they are lonely.

One of my students writes, "School is teaching us to be dependent on technology rather than each other," and those words render *me* speechless. I am poised to say, "Can we talk?" but I think I would amend that to, "We *have to* talk—now." We as teachers must find a way to get our students talking with us, with one another, and ultimately with a wider world. We need to give them the chance to experience the connection and comfort that conversation can bring. To do that, and to be passionate in our quest to change our classrooms, we need first to face the reality of the problem, and we need to make sure our students face that too.

I would ask that you pause a moment to watch a short spoken word performance. Gary Turk's "Look Up" first appeared on YouTube in April 2014 and immediately became an extraordinary internet success.

There is a curious irony here that a five-minute video performance speaking out *against* smartphones and the use of social media became a media success, but Turk clearly understands both that irony and the power of the media, and he uses it to make his audience, particularly younger viewers, think about the negative consequences of total immersion in an internet world. His poem cries out to viewers to put down their phones, look up into the world, and make a true human connection. Though scholars and scientists have offered similar sage advice, it's the emotional appeal of this video that works.

Watching the video, I am transported back to the summer of 2019 when I was in Paris, participating in a writing workshop. I traveled without a smartphone, well aware of the supposed "disadvantages" of doing so. No GPS, no French translator, no restaurant reviews, no bite-sized bits of tourist info. My workshop mates were by turns amused, befuddled, and stunned, and more than once they looked amazed when I met them at a café at the agreed upon time. "How did you find it without a phone?" they'd ask. I became "The Woman without a Smartphone," which, I admit, I held as a badge of honor. The point is, I wanted to experience Paris. I didn't want to constantly have to remind myself to "look up." For years, long before anyone ever owned a smartphone, I had traveled throughout Europe, often with a guidebook, sometimes with a map, and always with my words. And it was through my words, even in another language, that I made the best memories.

So too on this trip. On an early Sunday morning in search of the church of Saint-Sulpice, I encountered an elderly gentleman with a blue bow tie and a small white dog who valiantly tried to decipher my poor French and then led me through the winding streets to the wide doors of the church, where he motioned for me to hold his dog while he went in to light a candle. On another evening, a young woman with a wide smile shook her head when, with a question in my voice, I named a particular restaurant, and she pointed me instead to a tiny bistro, which I'm certain was much better than my choice would have been. And by day four and after much bumbling conversation, the woman who cleaned my room began to show me pictures of her children. As I wandered around the city, I didn't spend my time snapping pictures (in truth, I knew I could count on my new friends and their social media sites for that), but instead tried to connect with my surroundings and the people within them. As Turk says, "You don't need to stare at your menu, or at your contact list, / just talk to one another, and learn to co-exist." Though some might think that is an especially formidable task in a foreign country, I think I'd say it's becoming no easier here in the United States and in the more intimate spaces in which we live. Simply put, actual human connection through face-to-face conversation challenges many of us, and some of the greatest challenges we experience are in our classrooms.

One issue I need to address here is terminology. Is there a difference between *conversation* and *discussion*? What about *dialogue*? Is one more formal than another? What should we be doing in our classrooms? Conversing? Discussing? Dialoguing? To me personally, discussion sounds quite serious, conversation much more pleasant, and dialogue, well, a bit new age-ish. And then there are "academic conversations," what Jeff Zwiers in *Next Steps with Academic Conversations* describes as "powerful ways to develop students' content understandings, thinking skills, and language" (5). I wrestled with this issue of word choice as I began writing this book, and more than once I replaced one word with another with some sort of meaningful intention. But then I read *Discussion as a Way of Teaching* by Stephen D. Brookfield and Stephen Preskill. In the opening pages, the authors make a convincing case for recognizing the ways in which the three—discussion, conversation, and dialogue—blend, and they conclude that human connection is the goal, no matter what the word: "We define discussion as an alternately serious and playful effort by a group of two or more to share views and engage in mutual and reciprocal critique" (6). They go on to say, "Discussion is an important way for people to affiliate with one another, to develop the sympathies and skills that make participatory democracy possible" (7).

So, I decided, call it conversation, discussion, dialogue, whatever. The important point is that young people today need opportunities to experience the connection that talking to one another brings. Contemporary society offers them few opportunities—and many distractions. We are raising a generation for whom face-to-face communication is alien and intimidating. This reality and the consequences of it are startling and should concern every one of us as educators. Only when we recognize the problem do we have it in our power to alleviate it.

What Students Tell Us

Everything becomes a little different as soon as it is spoken out loud.

—Hermann Hesse

"Once it got going, a conversation seemed to run itself, swooping and gliding like the planchette of a Ouija board" (Gordon 85). Could there be a better image of good conversation? When I read that line in Emily Fox Gordon's essay "How I Learned to Talk," I was immediately carried back to a moment in my classroom when my students and I were suddenly swept up in words like that swooping planchette, one that had sat motionless for months. Perhaps we too were all searching for answers.

It had been a long, silent semester, me prompting and pleading for participation, my students reticent and reserved. There seemed to be no apparent reason for this struggle. These were college-bound sophomores, bright and hard-working, as the grades on their written work reflected. But they didn't talk. They sat quietly, they listened to me, they took notes assiduously, and when the bell rang, they clapped their notebooks shut and disappeared out the door. I'd end each period feeling like a mediocre stand-up comic, not bad enough to merit boos but unable to provoke a reaction from the audience. And then one day my students and I had a conversation about conversation—and the words began to fly. It was a discussion prompted less by my desperation than by my curiosity; I just wanted to know why they were so quiet. After so much silence, I didn't expect them to change, but I did want to know what they thought about talking, in class or out of class. I wanted to understand how they viewed this most basic form of human communication—and why it was missing in our classroom.

Except suddenly it wasn't. There I was, leaning against the file cabinet, looking out at all twenty-seven faces, when I heard myself say, "Talk to me about talking. What's up with conversation these days?" Then, strangely, hands began popping up all over the room, and there were those who couldn't even contain themselves long enough to raise a hand and instead simply started to speak.

"Nobody talks anymore," declared Jaclyn, but I couldn't quite tell if that was a lament or a simple statement of fact.

"That's because nobody wants to listen," a boy across the room called out, and though his classmates chuckled, I again wasn't sure how to interpret his words. Was he just being funny, or was it the truth?

"We don't need to talk. We text and stuff," said Ella.

"Yeah, it's so much easier," the student sitting next to her said, and all around the room heads nodded in agreement.

"I don't think I know how to talk," Sean announced, and more laughter erupted from the group. "That's what my parents say, anyway. They say I'll never get a job, never be able to do an interview." He looked glum briefly, but then brightened. "But hey, they're always on their phones and they got jobs. None of us talk to each other anyway."

"You're lucky!" This from Nina. "My parents make me talk. We have to put our phones away at dinner. We have to have *family* conversation." She rolled her eyes.

"Well, I talk to my friends . . . sometimes," a girl in the front ventured. "But in school, no one talks."

"Teachers don't even want kids to talk." This pronouncement came from the back of the room.

I was about to jump in here, to explain that I'd been trying desperately to get them to talk since September, but the metaphorical planchette was skittering across the board, and they were on to a different idea.

"When you talk, you can sound stupid," Annie said to a loud murmur of approval, and I wished I could point out the irony there. She spoke, and apparently her classmates saw her as smart. But at this point I didn't want to interrupt what seemed to be almost a miracle. The class was talking. So I leaned back and listened.

For a while the comments were random. They came from all corners of the room, spilling out of my students' mouths, and it seemed these were thoughts they had held in for too long.

"I used to talk in elementary school, but not anymore."

"I don't talk in school because I know I'll be wrong."

"My mom says that kids used to talk on the phone for hours. That's so weird."

"I feel like I don't know very many words."

I'm not sure I would call this conversation, as there was less swooping and gliding than there was lunging and leaping, but it was a start and an astounding change from the stony silence I was used to. So astonished was I by this outpouring of ideas that I forgot to monitor the time, and suddenly the bell rang. The students looked as surprised as I, and, even as they hurried to pack up their things, I heard them continuing to talk about talk.

As they were going out the door, I made a quick decision. "We're going to continue with this tomorrow," I called over their chatter. "Your assignment is to think about all you heard today and what you believe about conversation. Please really think about this!"

I took the few minutes before the next class to sit at my desk and wonder about what had just happened. How could it be that the best (the only?) conversation we'd had all year was one about conversation? And what were the chances it would happen again?

But it did. The next morning my students trooped into class, many of them looking expectant.

"Hey, are we gonna do that thing we did yesterday?" Sean asked.

I refrained from noting that "that thing" was talking. "Yes," I said. "I've been looking forward to it. How about all of you?"

There was much nodding and murmuring, and before I could suggest that we try to remember where we left off, Ella jumped in.

"Last night I was talking to my mother" (*Talking to her mother?* Again I showed restraint and didn't shout "Hallelujah!"), "and she said that when she was a kid, she and her friends talked all the time. We don't do that anymore. Even me and my best friends. I don't have conversations with them that last even four minutes."

I'm not sure of the significance of the four-minute mark, but I do know that her words set off a volley of comments, and immediately we were all engaged in a conversation with a clear connective thread. Students began to voice opinions about the importance or lack of importance of conversations among friends, and they began to offer ideas about why things have changed.

"Social media. It's much easier. You can talk to a bunch of people at once," a girl in Ella's camp said.

"But that's not real conversation," a boy responded. "That's just people hiding behind screens."

"Nah, I don't agree." Chase hadn't spoken much, but now he was vigorous in his opposition. "People always say that phones take away from face-to-face conversations. But that's not true. I've met a lot of people because of my phone. And when I'm hanging out with my friends, I might not look at my phone for hours."

Was I imagining it, or was there an almost audible gasp from some corners? Not look at your phone for hours?

The conversation continued for the entire period, with most of the class participating. I said very little, asking only for a point of clarification here or there, generally for my own benefit as someone not entirely familiar with the attitudes and behavior of my students' generation. At some point, the conversation moved naturally to conversation in the classroom, and students began to voice their fear of judgment and their anxiety about being wrong and sounding stupid. Today I was paying better attention to the clock, and as the minutes of class wound down, I told students to continue to think more about all the ideas they had heard and expressed so that tomorrow they could do some freewriting to synthesize and fully reflect on their ideas. I wanted the chance to reflect on their ideas as well.

"That was fun," Annie announced as they all started gathering their things. "We should have discussion more often."

Call it a teachable moment—for them and me. "But that's what I've been trying to do all year," I said. "I've been trying to get all of you to talk to each other and to get everyone involved."

Some of them looked at me quizzically, an unspoken "You have?" on their faces.

"When I ask you about Walter Younger and what it means to him to be a man, or why the Wingfield family is so caught up in dreams, I'm trying to get you to discuss ideas."

"Yeah, but those things have *answers*." This again from Sean. "I don't always know the answers."

"Because you don't always read the book," one of his buddies cracked.

Sean laughed good-naturedly and shrugged. "Whatever," he said. "But this is different. This is just our opinions. We don't have to know anything."

Had the bell not rung at that very second, I would have told him that you *do* have to know something. You have to know what you believe, and you have to know how to put your beliefs into words, and all of that is far more important than being able to summarize the plot of a play. But right now it was too late, so that would have to wait until after they wrote about conversation and I read their pieces and we talked once again.

And so conversation about conversation was born in my classroom and finds its way to this book.

Much of what I've learned about conversation in the classroom comes directly from my students, and so this knowledge is likely to change as society and the human interactions that are a part of it change. Certainly, as the research explored in Chapter 2 indicates, this would be an entirely different book had I written it prior to the appearance of the iPhone in 2007. This book is already somewhat different from the book I envisioned in 2019, months before either the COVID-19 pandemic or the social and political protests that shook the country. These events have changed all of us as individuals as well as the systems and structures we base our lives on. So I would not be at all surprised if other world-changing events, events that profoundly affect how we interact with one another, occur before this book ever finds its way into publication. But no matter when a book on conversation is written and no matter what the state of the world is at the moment it is read, the simple fact is that, as human beings with the capacity for conversation, we possess, as Celeste Headlee explains in *We Need to Talk: How to Have Conversations That Matter*," a uniquely human skill[,] . . . a compelling force behind our success as a species and our ascent up the food chain" (3). Some, like me, may bemoan what appears to be dwindling interest in conversation, but the ability—and the desire—to talk to one another continues to exist—and, as I am discovering, when this opportunity to talk is taken away, we feel its loss.

I had been asking my students to reflect, both orally and in writing, on the topic of conversation well before COVID-19 closed schools and dramatically changed the way students learned. But, as the school year wound down in June 2020, after three months of remote learning, I asked students for further thoughts on the importance—or lack of importance—of conversation in the classroom. I sent them the following assignment:

> I'd like you to write a reflection focused on *conversation in the classroom*. I'm curious as to how students view conversation these days. Though I'm specifically thinking about conversation in the classroom, you can certainly write about talking to others in general. I'm also wondering about remote learning, and since you are the experts (and guinea pigs!) on that, I want to know if and how the lack of "in person" conversation among students and teachers and other students affects your learning. Anything you have to say on the topic of conversation will be really helpful to me. This can simply be a freewrite. It will not be graded, and it does not demand any real polishing. You can make it an anonymous submission if you choose.

In many respects, the comments I received echoed in content the written reflections students had provided pre-COVID, but there was a difference in tone. Though students in both groups largely recognized the dearth of conversation in their classrooms and their lives in general, students in quarantine voiced a frustration and a despondency that I hadn't heard in the writing of students from months earlier. Perhaps it was simply the weariness we were all feeling after weeks of tedium coupled with anxiety, but I think there was more to it. Isolated—and with plenty of time to think—these teenagers became aware of the effect this lack of true human interaction was having on them, both as students and as human beings. As one student wrote:

> I feel that conversations in person is one of the main factors we lost through this quarantine online learning. It's actually pretty funny when I think of it, all these years of hating going to classes to hear lectures and taking notes, all I wanted to do was be done with them. To never have to sit through a 45-minute class again, but, since remote learning has started, all I wanted was to be in that class again, half asleep, trying to keep my eyes open enough that I don't get yelled at. There was something about being in the classroom and hearing the teacher explain it in person that just made learning a lot easier for me. I could stay on track a lot better and know what assignments I had for each class, and not only that, but if I had a question, it was a simple raise of the hand and wait to be called on where now I feel like I basically need to write a short story just to email the teacher about a question I have and wait for a specific day and time to get on Zoom with them to ask a question. Before quarantine life was a lot more simple and I think I speak for a majority of people when I say that I just want this online learning over with so I can go back to class and be surrounded by others all wanting to learn the same thing.

"Surrounded by others all wanting to learn the same thing." That, I think, is a pretty good definition of education when it works best, and it's an opportunity my students seemed to mourn the loss of. As one senior explained,

> Another thing that I do not like about remote learning is the disconnect from peers in the classroom. I feel that I learn better with other people around me so if I am struggling, I can ask, "What do you think of . . ." or similar questions. Overall, I think that learning in the classroom with discussion with others and the teacher is more productive and beneficial than remote learning.

A classmate concurred but offered an even darker picture:

> As far as communication goes in a classroom setting, I believe it is a key aspect to being a successful team member and learner. However, the coronavirus and the transition to remote learning and quarantine has caused people to be stripped of the freedom of communicating with people and friends face to face. If I was to predict the future, I would say that when this virus is gone, many people, especially kids and teens, are going to be very antisocial due to the lack of communication they get from school.

And finally, an eloquent reflection that made me very sad, sad that my students missed the experience of sharing together a play as beautiful as *Fences* and sad that they felt so separated from those of us who want so much to help them learn:

> If we didn't have an avenue of learning other viewpoints on a piece of literature, we would all end up in an echo chamber of our own interpretations which is always a real shame. However, that's what remote learning has kind of resulted in, as I didn't really feel like I was getting the benefit of hearing other voices and that made reading *Fences* a bit more difficult. I ended up understanding the book after a few re-reads of certain scenes, but overall, I was really missing the ability to talk about the scenes with others. The last thing that I missed a lot from school was the ability to talk directly with teachers for clarification or help. Having to email questions in place of actually talking directly with instructors added a barrier that made it difficult to understand the material completely. While it may be easy to just send an email, it still felt like I was never gonna get as concise of a response as I would in person and that was something I truly missed since leaving school. All in all, I feel like remote learning has given me a newfound appreciation for being able to discuss with my peers in class and in person, and it makes me miss school that much more.

The pandemic was, as we heard again and again, an unprecedented event, and its effects, particularly in terms of human connection and interaction, are ones we hope students will never encounter again. But the decline in verbal communication, both in school and out, is not limited to that time period, as students can attest. Three excerpts from their reflections, written months before the pandemic, are a clear indication of that, and, I would say, a clear cause for concern:

> I definitely feel like we don't talk as much in school as we used to and it's a lot more silent solo work than learning with class discussion. . . . I see it most when walking to the bathroom during class because there are many rooms that I pass where I see kids just silently glued to their Chromebooks. . . . I get very anxious when I have to talk to adults or even my older cousins because I'm only really used to talking to people my age or online, and having to talk to adults in person and not over text freaks me out.

> I don't think people have enough conversation both inside and outside of class. For example, I went to my cousin's house in New York for a few days during vacation, and I remember walking into the living room and seeing everyone on their phones. My

entire family was sitting in silence scrolling away. We barely get to see that side of the family, so it made me upset that no one was actually spending time with the family. I feel like this happens too often. Whenever I hang out with my friends, two of them are on their phones. . . . I was taught that when you are around people that it's rude to be on your phone. That's why it upsets me so much. I think everyone could benefit from putting the technology down and having a face to face conversation with someone.

I think that technology/texting makes it hard to have a normal conversation. Texting is carefree, short, to the point, and sometimes mindless, and it might be just me, but I'm terrible at carrying on a conversation in person. This maybe doesn't make sense, but that's as best as I can explain.

But it does make sense. It makes sense that when we as a society, and specifically when we as teachers, limit occasions for young people to engage in face-to-face conversation, they have fewer opportunities to hone their communication skills. Just as babies develop the ability to speak through repetition, practice, and, significantly, the praise and encouragement of those around them, so too do young people need many and varied low-risk chances to verbally interact with others if they are to learn to express themselves clearly, as well as to feel at ease in the exchange of ideas with others. When conversations are limited in society as a whole, it becomes our job as educators to provide consistent opportunities for students to engage in meaningful conversation in the classroom. And as hard as it is to keep a classroom full of twenty-first-century students engaged in conversation, we have to keep trying. Sometimes, as I well know, it seems easier to give in. When a class is disinterested in a discussion, my instinct is to abandon it and move to another activity. In one telling piece, one of my students vividly describes this all too familiar situation: "But I just think that now when a teacher asks something and tries to make it an open conversation, it is common for the room to go silent as everyone stares at their desks and the teacher sits in silence for a painful minute until they finally say something to wrap it up and continue teaching."

I know I've experienced more than one such "painful minute" and have, as a result, let my students off the hook. I can almost hear myself saying, "Okay, well, it doesn't seem as if anyone has much to say today. Maybe we should do some writing?" Not that there's anything wrong with doing some writing, and sometimes students can return to a conversation full of new ideas if they've had time to process their thoughts on paper. But when I or any other teacher routinely backs down from encouraging classroom conversation, we deprive our students of the chance to improve their skills as both speakers and listeners. The world today doesn't offer young people many chances to participate in conversation. So many human transactions are conducted via email or text, and I might note that, even in those interactions, students need help with communicating appropriately. I often shake my head when I open yet another email that begins, *Hey Ms. Rubenstein*. It's not that I demand formality, but I fear my students don't know that there are people and occasions that do. When it comes to verbal conversation, students first just need to do it more. As teachers, we know that consistent practice and repetition improve our students' reading and writing skills. The more they read, the better readers they become, and the more they write, the stronger their writing grows. So too is it true that the more students talk to one another, the better communicators they become, both as speakers *and* listeners. In the process, they develop skills that will serve them well, both professionally and personally in the adult world.

Why then is it so difficult to initiate fruitful conversation in our classrooms? When I was a student, I loved class discussion, partly, I suspect, because it saved me from taking notes on the teacher's lecture, but more because it was interesting and sometimes even exciting to hear my classmates' opinions. There was a rush and energy to our conversations on Kafka or Transcendentalism or Plath's poetry, and I remember our conversations spilling out the door and down the hall after the bell had rung. In my early years of teaching, I felt the same excitement in my students when we considered Hemingway's possible misogynism or Hawthorne's view of morality. It seemed that the challenge for a teacher in those years was to make sure that every student who wanted to speak had the opportunity, as so many hands were waving in the air and students were so eager to respond to their peers' comments. But times have changed, and it is important that teachers recognize how truly difficult conversation is for many students today. While we can decide to provide more opportunities for conversation, we need to also consider why students may not seize these opportunities. I see three main reasons for their reluctance, and I'll let my students' actions and words illustrate each.

#1: The Effect of a Distracted Attention Span

"Jimmy," I say, "for the last time, put that away." *That* is his phone. We're twenty-five minutes into the period, and this is the third time I've called him on it.

The first time he shoved the phone in his pocket. The second time he looked vaguely chagrined. Now, this third time, I'm met with the words, "Why? I'm paying attention." And it occurs to me that in the way we as a society have come to "pay attention," perhaps he is in fact doing so. Isn't multitasking what we're all about? But I try to put that train of thought on pause.

"Jimmy, just put your phone on the floor for five minutes," I say. I know I should simply take it away, but frankly I'm curious to see if he's even able to put it down. When he balks, I resort to the threat, ". . . or else I'm taking it away."

He sighs. "Okay," he says and puts the phone close to his sneakered foot. "Time me."

I do, and with one eye on the clock, the other on Jimmy, and my mind on the class discussion (now who's multitasking?), we all resume talking, but barely a minute goes by when I see Jimmy looking down, reaching down, and then suddenly swooping up the phone. He's not being recalcitrant. He can't help himself, and I'm reminded once again of the powerful hold technology has over our students and its ability to distract them from any other sort of activity. Students in the classroom have always been distractible, but what I see as different now is that (1) they truly believe they can give partial attention to a multitude of activities without negative impact, and (2) virtually *nothing* holds their attention for long, even that which technology offers, as the constant scrolling and clicking indicate. Yet in this climate and faced with these hurdles, we strive to get them to talk to one another.

Good conversation is a slow process and one that involves discoveries we make as we hear and consider the ideas of others. We speak glibly about "the art of conversation," without perhaps acknowledging that, as with all art forms, the creation of good conversation takes time, patience, and commitment. As Catherine Blyth explains in *The Art of Conversation*, "[Conversation] takes two or more people and two things: attention and interest" (14). These days the first is hard to come by. We know it by our classroom experience, but research adds an interesting twist:

> The average attention span for the notoriously ill-focused goldfish is nine seconds, but according to a new study from Microsoft Corp., people now generally lose concentration after eight seconds, highlighting the effects of an increasingly digitalized lifestyle on the brain.
>
> Researchers in Canada surveyed 2,000 participants and studied the brain activity of 112 others using electroencephalograms (EEGs). Microsoft found that since the year 2000 (or about when the mobile revolution began) the average attention span dropped from 12 seconds to eight seconds. (McSpadden)

This may not sound like much, but when we are struggling to get students to "Pay attention!" to the thread of a discussion, seconds matter.

As annoyed as I may get when students begin riffling through their backpacks, whispering to one another, or surreptitiously checking their phones while one of their classmates is speaking, I try to remind myself that they are not being intentionally rude. They just don't know how to focus their attention, and so they lose interest in the conversation and want to move on to something new.

I frequently see my students grow impatient with discussion, and more than once one has asked irritably, "So what's the answer?" It's difficult for them to understand that you can't Google everything and that some ideas and "answers" only arise when people offer half-formed thoughts that others welcome and build upon. Teenagers are so used to the speed of so much in our contemporary, fast-paced world that face-to-face conversation can feel slow and purposeless to them, and this contributes to our struggle to keep them focused and engaged in class discussion. Just as language has in effect become stunted by the demands of technology, so too have our students' conversational skills been stunted by their reliance on technology. For most of them, communication should be, as the student above described, "short, to the point," the language of the text screen, and as such completely different from the slow pace and rambling style of much conversation. I admit, it cheers me when I read a rare comment such as this from a student: "People that text the way they talk are people I tend to stay in contact with the most. People that text very casually come off as uninterested, and I stop trying because it seems like they don't care. Conversation can be nerve wracking and awkward, but essential to life in my personal opinion." Actual conversation demands attention in order to follow the threads of speakers' ideas and to interpret underlying emotions, the latter skill one with which many young people especially struggle. As one student writes, "It's hard to read emotions in text conversations." Another notes, "Now with remote [learning], not only can you not ask teachers questions face to face, but often when you email them it is hard to understand what they mean sometimes due to the absence of an inflection in their voice." Focused attention, attention that appreciates nuances, is not the forte of this generation. They have been raised to admire the ability to multitask, and they are not alone. Despite evidence that indicates the negative outcome of multitasking, we all engage in it, and we often pride ourselves on our ability to "get so much done"—or so we think:

> But in this, we pursue an illusion. When we think we are multitasking, our brains are actually moving quickly from one thing to the next, and our performance degrades for each new task we add to the mix. . . . We've seen that not only do multitaskers have trouble deciding how to organize their time, but over time, they "forget" how to read human emotions. Students—for example, my students—

> think that texting during class does not interrupt their understanding of class conversation, but they are wrong. The myth of multitasking is just that: a myth. (Turkle 213)

The students Sherry Turkle, an expert on technology and its effects on human relationships, refers to are her seminar students at Massachusetts Institute of Technology, presumably more motivated than many of our high school students. Still, even for them, there is a competition between class conversation and the lure of technology. Though we *might* in our high school classrooms be able to control, to some extent, the use of cell phones and computers, we all know that students are perennially involved in activities that are not the focus of the day's lesson, and for them that is simply the norm. Today a teacher's command to "Put that away"—whether "that" be homework for history class, a phone in a lap, or a tube of mascara—is frequently met with the same bewilderment Jimmy expressed. Why can't they be doing two or three or four things at once? Isn't that just the way we get things done in our world? Maybe in some instances it is, but not, as Turkle explains, in terms of conversation. This sort of "distracted attention" is counterproductive to real conversation because, "To converse, you don't just have to perform turn taking, you have to listen to someone else, to read their body, their voice, their tone, and their silences" (45). In other words, productive and meaningful conversation demands serious attention to all aspects of those with whom you are conversing. You can't just hear their words; you need to "see" those words—and feelings—through body language. You need to listen carefully to the pitch of the voice, which sometimes doesn't match the words being spoken. You need to process and interpret the pauses and silences. Moreover, as an active participant in the conversation, you need to be fully present if you are to communicate your own thoughts in any meaningful way. How often in classrooms do students repeat something that was just said or ask a question that was just answered, all because they weren't paying attention? Conversation in classrooms has become something of a novelty these days, and some students think of it as "downtime" and a "break" from learning. But the more they engage in it, the more they realize how much effort each participant must give to the conversation and how profound the human connection that results can be.

I'd like to think that this sort of realization can extend beyond the classroom and have a positive effect on teenagers' wider social interactions. One of the most startling facts I discovered when researching the topic of conversation was something that I knew intuitively from my own experience but had never before seen verified. This involves the presence of cell phones when people are engaged in face-to-face conversation. We all know how annoying it is to have a conversation interrupted when our conversational partner abandons us for a ringing cell phone, but what strikes me as even more unnerving is what the simple *presence* of a phone does to negatively impact meaningful conversation:

> Studies show that the mere presence of a phone on the table (even a phone turned off) changes what people talk about. If we think we might be interrupted, we keep conversations light, on topics of little controversy or consequence. And conversations with phones on the landscape block empathic connection. If two people are speaking and there is a phone on a nearby desk, each feels less connected to the other than when there is no phone present. *Even a silent phone disconnects us.* (Turkle 21)

If students had their way in class, they would likely never put their phones down. My students are allowed to have their phones in class, but they must keep them off unless a teacher gives permission to use them for a particular purpose. Now, considering these studies, I think it's even more important that phones be completely out of sight. We know that for some students, certainly for Jimmy, their attachment to their phone borders on addiction, but it seems that for all of us, a phone becomes a barrier to the kind of conversation and human connection we want to nurture in our classrooms. We need to do everything we can to reduce the distractions for our students and to help them develop the ability to truly engage with others face to face. As one of my students writes, "I think people are talking less because they are more focused on their needs, what they want. . . . I think it's harder for people to have conversations because they are doing it less and focusing only on what they want."

In a sort of aside, I'd add this—our students are not the only ones who become "distracted." Even as teachers committed to a path defined by what we believe our students need, we sometimes fall victim to the "hurry up" culture and try to do too much too fast. Faced with tightly packed curricula, we feel pressured to "move along" in order to get our students to reach the next step, the next skill, the next level. This pressure, combined with our concern about losing many class periods to mandated testing and other "essentials" ordered by administrators and state requirements, causes us to feel we can't quite justify time spent on conversation and extended discussion, the sort of thing we can't easily assess, check off our list, and call "done." As a result, we often don't encourage students to explore ideas through conversation, but instead supply the material we think they need and move on. In the process, our classrooms and our students suffer.

#2: Fear of Failure

"Casey," I write in the margins of a purple striped notebook, "you have such great things to say in this journal. How come you don't share some of this in class?" Okay, so I know this is basically a rhetorical question. This journal is a composite of Casey's reactions to the readings and discussion we've been having in our Contemporary American Culture class. I don't expect her to respond to my question—even though I wish she would. But this doesn't stop me from writing these sorts of comments in students' journals, or from thinking about the reasons these insightful writers don't speak up in class. I suspect we've all been surprised by the startlingly perceptive comments that can pop up in students' journals or reading logs and have thought about how much their ideas would have contributed to the class discussion—had the writers been willing to share them. And I know that though no doubt Casey and others like her appreciate my positive comments, my words won't necessarily make a difference when it comes to the next opportunity to share their thoughts. It's likely Casey will continue to sit there silently while the discussion falters, perhaps replaying her thoughts in her head, but staying silent. As students tell me repeatedly when I push them to explain why they don't speak up to share their ideas, they are simply afraid of being "wrong."

Students have always been afraid of being wrong. It takes confidence to offer up an opinion or answer in front of your peers, and it's certainly easy to understand why it seems more appealing to many students to just keep quiet. One of my sophomores begins a reflection with these lines, "Classroom-wise I believe there's less conversation because less people are confident. People are scared to raise their hand and answer a question because they think everyone will think they're dumb if they answer it wrong. If they ask a question, they're scared it will be a stupid question."

While students in previous decades might have written these same words, research indicates that there's an additional problem, particular to the present social and educational climate. A student describes it this way: "I don't usually talk in class because I don't like being blatantly wrong. I'm still learning and taking in information, but I just don't have the confidence to actually say what I'm thinking. I think this is because we've kind of been brought up in such a way that there's one answer and if you get it wrong, you have to fix it."

In her book *iGen*, Jean M. Twenge offers evidence of this situation. Twenge's work studies young people born between 1995 and 2012, those students graduating from high school between 2012 and 2030. This is a book I strongly suggest every teacher read, as it offers a vivid portrait of this generation in all areas of their lives, as well as guidance to help the rest of us understand these young people. Twenge discusses changes in learning styles of this generation, the iGen'ers:

> iGen'ers are more hesitant to talk in class and to ask questions—they are scared of saying the wrong thing and not as sure of their opinions. (When McGraw-Hill Education polled more than six hundred college faculty in 2017, 70% said students were less willing to ask questions and participate in class than they were five years ago.) It takes more reassurance and trust to get them to actively participate in class. (307)

Saying the "wrong thing" can have two very different meanings, the second of which I discuss in #3 below, but here the focus is on the fear of being "incorrect." This is a fear that can, in part at least, be attributed to the effect standardized testing has had on this generation of students. Our students have been raised to believe in one correct answer. When they prep and practice for state-mandated testing, they are trained to find the right response; creative thinking is not encouraged. More than once I've found myself trying to defend the "correct" answer on a Massachusetts Comprehensive Assessment System (MCAS) practice test, when I, like the original thinker sitting in the front row of my classroom, can definitely see the validity of a different response. For the most part, I try to avoid asking questions in class that do have only one correct answer, recognizing moreover that this factual material ("How does Mrs. Mallard react to the news that her husband is alive in Kate Chopin's 'The Story of an Hour'?"; "What's the difference between ethos and pathos?"; "Give an example of metonymy in 'kitchenette building' by Gwendolyn Brooks.") is not the stuff of good conversation. It's far better to ask students why they think O. E. Parker is so driven to get tattoos in Flannery O'Connor's "Parker's Back," to describe the feeling of sunlight, or to consider the levels of symbolism of Kamala's bird in the golden cage in *Siddhartha*. But even when the question or discussion prompt welcomes a wide range of responses, it's still easy for students to fear that their particular response will be seen as a foolish one. As one student explains, "Sometimes the kids don't participate. I feel that's because we feel pressured to be cool or answer right. Maybe we're all more socially conscious because of social media, I don't know. There is a lot of pressure."

There *is* a lot of pressure, and to ease the pressure that students feel to be "right," it's important for us to be encouraging toward *every* serious response that students offer in class conversation. Although it's true that we often disparage the present culture that awards every child a trophy in virtually every endeavor they undertake, I'm not so sure that we as teachers are always quick to applaud our students' verbal efforts in the classroom, perhaps because we forget what a tremendous risk some students feel they take when they put a hand up in the air. It can be difficult at times to offer praise of a teenager's comments without that praise sounding inflated or making the student feel self-conscious. Somehow, no matter what the time period, it's never been considered entirely "cool" to participate in class. But as Twenge points out, students need reassurance in order to feel comfortable speaking up in class. A comment that comes out of the proverbial left field may suddenly provoke an entirely new way of looking at a topic, and a comment that stirs controversy may keep the conversation alive. So too do questions, even ones that many students may already know the answer to, promote more conversation. Certainly, as teachers we need to work to help our students engage in increasingly *productive* conversation, but, until students are willing to share whatever ideas they have, there will be no conversation at all. So we must first create an environment where students feel safe sharing their opinions and asking their questions. We all know the students who are always eager to make their voices heard, and we all know those who happily sit back and let them. Our task is to encourage as many students as possible to share the time we have for conversation. A good teaching day for me is when a student who rarely speaks suddenly has something to say—and their classmates listen. That, I believe, is a good learning day for all of us.

But not all days are good learning days for our students, as the following writer points out. These words shook me and made me wonder how many times I was guilty of this impatience and frustration—and how many conversations I had squelched in the process:

> Teachers sometimes get mad when we ask questions at all. I sometimes will ask more about a certain topic, and the response is, "You should have learned this last year. I'm not teaching it to you again." I've gotten this response a lot and it makes me not want to ask questions. It makes me just want to suffer through silently rather than "disrupt" the class by asking a question.

How sad is it that students view the act of asking a question—and likely promoting a conversation—as causing a disruption, but that is what their experience has taught them. In an earlier portion of the reflection, this same student wrote, "[Teachers] say things like, 'You should have been listening,' or 'You're a sophomore. You should be able to figure it out.'" Clearly these are the kind of comments that effectively shut down conversation. Sure, kids should be listening, and sure, they likely have been taught certain things before, but if they are searching for answers, they're at least open to genuine communication. I think sometimes of things that I good-naturedly tolerate in conversations I have with friends—the repetition of ideas, an irrelevant comment, a bit of stage stealing—and I wonder why I often feel exasperated by students who do the same things. Perhaps I too am a product of a culture that pushes students to find the right answer and to find it fast, and, as a result, I lose patience and fail to offer students the encouragement they need to speak up. But I know that it's up to me, and to every classroom teacher, not only to offer this encouragement but also to serve as a model listener, giving each student's words the respect and consideration they deserve. And if some students make a face, groan, or guffaw when a classmate speaks, it is absolutely my responsibility to quash that behavior. My approach isn't to sternly call out such an ill-mannered student with a sharp "Stop that!" sort of command (which only calls more attention to the rude behavior and likely embarrasses the original speaker), but rather to pull that student into the conversation.

So, when Alex makes it all too clear that he thinks what Krista has said is stupid, I turn to him and say, "Alex, you seem to have a different perspective on this than Krista. What are you thinking?" In the best-case scenario, he's thinking something that *does* move the discussion along, but if he's thinking nothing other than critical thoughts about his classmate's words and falls silent, then perhaps he'll think twice before making those thoughts public again.

As teachers we must do our best to create a risk-free classroom environment where students feel comfortable expressing their ideas and asking their questions, but we also need to be realistic enough to accept that not all students will choose to be actively engaged in class conversation. Reading students' final reflections in June 2020, I realized that for a small group of students, three months of online learning had provided a blessed respite. As one student wrote:

> In terms of conversation—both in the classroom and in the social community—it can be important but not always the easiest outcome to achieve. For students like myself who are highly introverted, quiet and spend our time listening, it is a bit out of our comfort zone to need to speak out in the classroom (or in most situations). I think that "cold-calling" and forceful participation by voice is not effective in the classroom. Instead, it is a major source of daily anxiety for some people. Going back to myself, it puts me on edge, causes a need for on-the-spot thinking (resulting in a lack of composure), and is a major cause for anxiety in all classes. With the current remote learning situation, it both makes school harder and easier in [the] context of conversation. It makes it harder (nearly impossible) to get the complete and direct help from staff and teachers, as well as getting extra help. It does, on the other hand, give the students like me a break from worrying about having to talk in class.

Students like this writer are not just afraid of being wrong when they speak in class; they are afraid of speaking at all. I believe it's important that we respect the qualities of an introvert, just as we respect all students' differences. A compassionate teacher can tell the difference between a student who is simply hesitant to talk and needs some support to do so versus one whose entire nature is opposed to any sort of public speaking. I see no benefit whatsoever to putting a student in the latter group on the spot through cold-calling or the like, and I trust this writer (and those like her) when she writes, "One major thought that comes to mind, and generally always has for my schooling career, is this: just because we are not talking or volunteering to participate, does not mean we are not engaged and learning."

Engagement—this is what I seek through conversation in my classroom, and I am willing to recognize that it comes in different forms. But my goal is to give students the opportunity to develop their unique skills as speakers *and* listeners in a safe environment, one in which there is no shame in being wrong. When that happens, we all benefit, from those with the loudest voices to those with the softest.

#3: Fear of Giving Offense

But what is a safe environment these days? I have students who preface virtually everything they say with the phrase, "I don't want to offend anyone . . ."—and I have students who, from the moment they open their mouths, consistently use words, body language, and tone to express the opposite. This second group I can deal with most of the time. Courtesy and civility are on my side, and I feel justified in telling them to tone it down. Dealing with the former group is different, and it grows more challenging each year.

We live in a time when it's easy to offend, even when there is no such intent. The "rules" seem to change almost daily, and these days I find myself in class passing the words in my head by a sort of self-censor before I say them aloud. Fortunately, the censor rarely has to stop me, but I'm cautious in these times because language has become so charged. For the most part, this is a good thing. Thoughtless use of language can do irreparable damage and can certainly perpetuate prejudices and divisions that we must all fight against. But, for many of our students, this "PC culture," as they call it, is extremely intimidating, and they find it difficult to honestly express themselves within it. As one student laments,

> In today's society it's hard to express your opinion in the classroom. There's always going to be someone who disagrees. People could find your opinion offensive and get critical and upset. It's their way or the highway. You can't talk about politics because everyone gets upset with your beliefs, so it's better to just say nothing at all. You can feel attacked by others when they comment on your views.

This writer is not alone. These sorts of feelings are echoed in many of my students' reflections:

> I don't talk much in class any more due to how judged I feel when I speak my mind.

> It's easy to offend some people, so I have to be really careful. I can't act like myself sometimes.

> People lie through their teeth constantly, and many important conversations are diluted and censored to remain "polite" and "politically correct." What this does is hide truths and doesn't let any positive changes occur. In fact, any changes. . . . Conversations have become bland and unimportant.

Such are the times in which we and our students live, and this fear of giving offense creates an enormous challenge for us in terms of classroom conversation. Chapter 6, "'We Need to Talk': Navigating Difficult Conversations," considers in much more depth the challenge of holding difficult conversations and offers suggestions for doing so. But the primary point to consider here is that, in their attempt to not offend anyone, many students simply opt out of the conversation, especially—and unfortunately—when that conversation tackles a controversial issue. As a teacher, it's vital to continually reassure students that all opinions, expressed with civility, are welcome, and that it's only through the open sharing of conflicting ideas that we come to understand each other, and sometimes even modify our own views. Which all sounds fine until you're teaching a class that's just read "The Problem That Has No Name," an excerpt from Betty Friedan's *The Feminine Mystique*, and most of the boys in class are looking down at their desks because they know, they just know, that one wrong word and the wrath of fifteen senior girls will come down upon them.

"I'm just not gonna say anything," Brian says. He pauses for a second. "But—"

"But what?" I prompt. Everyone is watching him, and I see a couple of his buddies shake their heads, as if in silent warning. "Brian," I say, "if you have thoughts or questions, this is the place to express them. We're all here to share our ideas—and to learn from each other." I send a glance across the room, hoping to see agreement in the girls' faces. Most are just waiting, their expressions not welcoming.

"Okay, well, I don't want to get anyone mad at me, but I'm just gonna say it." His buddies groan and look at him woefully. "The thing is, girls are just better at taking care of kids. It's *nature.*"

It's also 2019 and, frankly, his words surprise me. Not surprisingly, there is a huge eruption from the female contingent, and words begin to fly, toppling over one another.

"That is *so* wrong. . . ."

"Having a kid isn't the same as raising a kid—"

"Why should women have to give up their careers for kids? Men don't."

"What do you think we are? Just babymakers?"

Brian gives me an *I told you so* look, but I know he's tough and can handle a bit of attack, so for a minute or two I let students air their immediate reactions, hoping that will decompress the situation enough to let us all step back to discuss the comments rationally. At the same time, I'm listening carefully to make sure none of the spontaneous outbursts attacks Brian personally. My students know that you can challenge someone's ideas, but you cannot make that attack personal.

Once calm is restored, I remind everyone that Brian has the right to his opinion, as does every student in the room, and I assure Brian that he's likely not alone in his beliefs and that I appreciate his willingness to express controversial views.

"It's only when we talk about things we believe that we can begin to find some points of shared consensus," I tell them. "I know it's hard to say what you believe when you know that many of those around you are in strong disagreement. But I also know, Brian, that your beliefs in this instance are not directed personally to anyone in this room, and I know you're not intending to anger or offend anyone. You have reasons for believing what you do, as do those who don't agree. So let's talk about those reasons."

My hope is that this sort of approach opens the door to one of those difficult—but necessary—conversations. For many adolescents, beliefs are often borrowed or handed down and, as a result, parroted without any real thought. At this moment, I don't know whether Brian has a real basis for his beliefs about women's roles based on his experience or some sort of knowledge, or whether he's simply repeating ideas he has heard and never questioned. It's only through serious conversation that students can begin to understand not only the opinions of others but, equally important, the reasons behind their own opinions. Yet it's vital that they explore ideas, especially unpopular ones, without offending others, making their disagreement constructive rather than destructive. This, I think, is best achieved through the teacher's guidance and modeling.

So Brian, his classmates, and I spend the period in conversation about male and female roles and the changes in these roles over time. We continue to refer back to Friedan's words, and we discuss the social implications of her work. We talk about nature versus nurture, and we share stories of our own upbringing. What we have is a civil conversation. It's not one intended to change any student's beliefs (even when you might just want to do so), but rather to provide a safe and open forum for the expression of beliefs and the opportunity to explore the rationale behind them. If students can leave the classroom still sharing thoughts and maybe even laughing—"Good luck on getting a prom date!" one of the senior girls teases Brian—then we have had a good class and a meaningful conversation.

This is an issue I explore further in Chapter 6, but it's important to emphasize here that, despite the friction inherent in a difficult conversation, teachers need to encourage students to pursue these serious conversations and to honestly express their thoughts and opinions. Teachers should also be willing to admit to their own concerns in terms of voicing ideas on sensitive topics. I want my students to understand that we are all learning to navigate our way in this quickly changing world, and that takes courage. I tell them to remember that the classroom *is* a place of learning, and one thing they will continue to learn is how to use language and express controversial views appropriately with respect to societal norms. It is far better for students to learn these lessons—and to make mistakes—in the relative safety of a high school classroom rather than in the wider adult world where the consequences are far more severe.

Another reason it's important for teachers to emphasize their commitment to a safe and open classroom is that students can mistakenly believe they can be penalized for holding views different from that of the teacher. In one student's words, "I believe a lot of kids don't talk because they fear judgment, from peers who might think they're weird and stupid and from teachers who may come to dislike them or give them a bad grade." In the very first days of class, I make it clear to students that, at various times, all of us will likely hold widely differing views, but that this is a safe space and that everyone's views deserve to be heard. I don't shy away from expressing my personal views when we discuss controversial topics, but I stress that these opinions in no way affect my feelings toward students who might disagree, nor do they ever impact students' grades. It is, of course, easy enough to say this, and I know that students will come to truly believe it only when I demonstrate it. I do that by always welcoming diverse opinions and encouraging intelligent questions that help students clarify their views for me and for their classmates. If there are moments in a class when it seems students are holding back, fearful of expressing what they believe, I might give them a few minutes to put their ideas on paper, and then I share these freewrites anonymously to get honest discussion going. Students quickly learn too that a well-written paper earns an A, whether I support its views or not, and, with the writer's permission, I often share such papers aloud with the class.

I truly appreciate the sentiment of that student who begins, "I don't want to offend anyone. . . ." I'd like to believe that most of us don't want to offend anyone, but it takes a remarkable blend of awareness, sensitivity, and diplomacy to avoid doing just that in many situations. For students soon to enter the adult world, the classroom may be their last opportunity to develop the skills necessary to engage honestly and positively with a wide and diverse world. If we, as educators, close off their opportunities for difficult conversation, we have narrowed their world and failed to give them the skills they need to make that world a better one.

I want to note one more thing that deeply impacts the potential for conversation in the classroom but that is out of the teacher's hands. This involves the home environment. Simply put, there are parents who encourage conversation within the family, and there are those who don't. Some students come to us from homes where conversation is an integral part of family life, while others live in families who, for a variety of reasons, do not make conversation a priority. Kids see the difference. Like Sean and Nina in the first part of this chapter, they recognize that in some families, parents work to make conversation happen (whether their children appreciate it or not!), while other parents are perhaps too busy or too overwhelmed by other family responsibilities to do so, or they may have fallen victim to the lure of technology themselves. One student writes, "In my house, my family is never really there. So we don't have many conversations," while another speaks regretfully of the increasing presence of technology:

> Conversations have gone away at home too. When I was younger I always went to a family friend's house. All of us would always play games or watch a movie together. However now I get to their house and all they want to do is sit on their phones. This is extremely annoying to me because I would enjoy playing a board game or just talking to them, but they can never focus due to the distraction of their phones.

As teachers, there is little we can do to change the quantity or quality of social interactions our students have within their families. I can, though, silently applaud the efforts of this father who, as his child writes, "will make my brothers and I talk to the cashier or place orders over the phone and usually won't answer texts unless they're important if we don't call because he says we never have any human interaction." That writer is lucky to have a parent committed to helping them learn the art of conversation. But for those students whose homes are silent, we in our classrooms offer what is likely the next best chance they have to develop conversational skills. In a time when so many responsibilities that once belonged to other factions of society are now being put on us as educators, it can be easy to think, "Oh no, not one more thing." But this one thing—this ability to converse with one another—is one very important thing. It's the thing that gives us our humanity and allows us to share ourselves fully with the world.

2

What Research Tells Us

Let us make a special effort to stop communicating with each other, so we can have some conversation.

—*Mark Twain*

For a long time, I believed that the struggle to get a group of students to talk about their reaction to a book, interpretation of a poem, or opinion on an issue was purely a classroom dilemma. I blamed it on (1) a disinterest in all things academic, (2) a fear of being "wrong," or (3) a case of burnout after too many hours in classrooms. In the earlier years of my career, I may have been right, but I think things are different now. As I listen (or attempt to listen) to students before class, after class, and in the hallways, I hear much of the same silence that greets me when I ask a question about Gatsby's motives, Toni Morrison's voice, or immigration policies. Spaces that were once filled with teenage talk, however inane it might have sometimes seemed, now are quiet.

This was brought home to me vividly just a couple of years ago when I met a new homeroom class of seventeen ninth graders. The weekly homeroom period was designed as a space where students could, in effect, take a breath—no assignments, no grades, no pressure. There were periodic visits by three senior mentors, and I was there to answer questions and help acclimate these ninth graders to their new, big, five-town school. Some students used this short period as a study hall and caught up with assignments, and a few went off to club meetings, but most sat absolutely silent, looking at their screens.

"Maybe it's because they're ninth graders," I mused. "They come from five different towns. They don't know each other. Maybe they're just awkward and a little uncomfortable." I tried to initiate conversations with them, sometimes in small groups, sometimes one on one. I tried to find connections among students ("Oh, do you both play volleyball?" "So, are you all in the same Spanish class?"), and though they were never rude nor hostile, they met all my overtures with a sort of weary reticence, the kind you would accord to the great-aunt who you wished would just leave you alone. And inevitably their eyes stayed fixed on their phones and Chromebooks. They were no different with the senior mentors, three exceptionally lively students whose mission was to offer advice and wisdom born of being experienced high schoolers, and who seemed utterly dejected by the lack of enthusiasm with which they were met. "They don't even want to play 7-Up," one sighed.

The situation didn't get any better. The year went on, and homeroom period loomed as a black hole of silence. I hoped that when I met these students again as their sophomore year began, things would be different, but they were not. And so I came to understand, this is a new breed of student, not necessarily better or worse but new and very different. These are young people for whom conversation is a lost art, an art they likely don't even realize is missing.

In *Reclaiming Conversation*, Sherry Turkle relates an anecdote about an experience she had while working on that book. She tells a twenty-six-year-old friend that she is writing a book on conversation: "His reaction is close to a snort: 'Conversation? It died in 2009'" (137).

I admit to imagining a similar reaction to this book. Conversation? In the classroom? Really? That point was brought home to me even more after months of remote learning, when it seemed we might never be in a classroom again, never mind conversing. But I take heart in the fact that, after months of remote learning, my students voiced how tired they were of computer screens and Google Meets and the stuff of a virtual world. This gives me hope that they may now greet good old-fashioned face-to-face conversation as something to embrace. But in truth the world is changing so rapidly that what we know (or think we know) of students today will likely be different in a very short space of time, and that includes their feelings about communication.

To offer further evidence of this, consider the findings of a two-part study conducted by Common Sense Research, part of Common Sense Media, a non-profit organization that explores the impact of technology and media on children. The first part of the study, "Social Media, Social Life: How Teens View Their Digital Lives, 2012," conducted in that year, involved 1,000 adolescents ages thirteen to seventeen (Rideout). The second part of the study, "Social Media, Social Life: Teens Reveal Their Experiences, 2018," conducted in the spring of 2018, involved a separate sample of 1,141 young people of the same age group. The surveys aimed to track social media use among American teenagers. Among the 2012 findings,

> Despite being avid social media users, talking to each other in person is still teens' favorite way to communicate. About half (49%) of all teens say their favorite way to communicate with their friends is in person. Texting is the next favorite (33%), with social networking (7%), talking on the phone (4%), and Twitter (1%) far behind.
>
> The main reasons kids prefer face-to-face conversations are that they're more fun (38%) and that they can understand what people really mean better in person (29%). The main reasons some kids prefer texting is that it's quick (30%) and easy (23%); others say it gives them more time to think about how to respond (16%) or is more private (11%). (Rideout)

Encouraging, yes? And to many of us, logical. Yet a mere six years later, the findings were quite different. The 2018 study revealed that 61 percent of teenagers preferred something other than face-to-face conversation ("Social Media"). "Most teens now say their favorite mode of communication is texting (35%), according to a new survey released Monday from Common Sense, a children's and media advocacy organization. Compared to 2012, much higher proportions selected social media (16%) and video chatting (10%), while less than one third said they prefer chatting with friends face-to-face" (Steinmetz).

In an equally telling finding from the 2018 report,

> The proportion of teens who use social media multiple times a day has doubled over the past six years: In 2012, 34 percent of teens used social media more than once a day; today, 70 percent do. . . . In fact, 38 percent of teens today say they use social media multiple times an hour, including 16 percent who say they use it "almost constantly." ("Social Media" 8)

It's worth noting too that teenagers in the 2018 study were not unaware of the effects of these changes:

> Teens are more likely to say they're distracted from personal relationships by social media today than they were in 2012: Fifty-four percent of teens agree that using social media "often distracts me when I should be paying attention to the people I'm with," up from 44 percent in 2012; and 42 percent agree that the time they spend using social media "has taken away from time I could be spending with friends in person," up from 34 percent six years ago. ("Social Media" 12)

Again, it's important to remember that this change occurred in a very short time period, the time, in fact, between the day a student enters seventh grade and the day they graduate from high school, six short years.

The year 2012 seems, in fact, to be the all-important year when the path toward change became evident, as Twenge discusses in depth in *iGen*:

> But around 2012, I started seeing large, abrupt shifts in teens' behaviors and emotional states. All of a sudden, the line graphs looked like steep mountains—rapid drop-offs erased the gains of decades in just a few years; after years of gradual inclines and hollows, sheer cliffs suddenly brought traits to all-time highs. In all of my analyses of generational data—some of it reaching back to the 1930s—I had never seen anything like it.
>
> At first, I wondered if these were random blips that would disappear after a year or two. But they didn't—the trends kept going, creating sustained, and often unprecedented, trends. As I dug into the data, a pattern emerged: many of the large changes began around 2011 or 2012. . . .
>
> Then it occurred to me: 2011–12 was exactly when the majority of Americans started to own cell phones that could access the Internet, popularly known as smartphones. The product of this sudden shift is iGen. (4)

These are our students. This is their generation, and the data support the changes Twenge describes and the speed of this ever-increasing technology. This is made clear by the 2018 study "Teens, Social Media and Technology 2018" conducted by the Pew Research Center. In one key finding, "Some 95% of teens now say that they have or have access to a smartphone, which represents a 22-percentage-point increase from the 73% of teens who said this in 2014–2015. Smartphone ownership is nearly universal among teens of different genders, races and ethnicities and socioeconomic backgrounds" (Anderson and Jiang).

An interesting point in this later study is that teenagers were not as apt to regard the effect of social media on their lives as negative. Forty-five percent of those surveyed called the effect neither positive nor negative, with 31 percent indicating that social media has a mostly positive impact and 24 percent seeing its effect as mostly negative (Anderson and Jiang). For these young people in 2018, it seems simply that social media was what it was—and it was definitely a significant element in their lives.

As teachers we need to be aware of how quickly our students' lives have changed and will continue to change in terms of technology—and how likely they are to simply accept whatever these changes are and go forward. It's difficult to bemoan what you're told you've lost if you never had it anyway. I can certainly sit in my homeroom and feel bereft that there is no chatty conversation, no spontaneous give and take, and no laughter, but these fourteen-year-olds have no reason to miss this kind of social interaction because they haven't experienced it. They get their social "fix" by scrolling through their phones, clicking here and clicking there. *FOMO* has a particular meaning for them, and it's not about missing out on conversation—unless we show them what in fact they are missing.

That is a central purpose of this book—to show teachers how we can bring conversation into the classroom to benefit not only our students' academic learning but also their social and emotional health, something we all are aware is increasingly in our hands.

In *Reclaiming Conversation,* Turkle describes a birthday party in the early years of the smartphone where a fifteen-year-old and her friends, male and female, gather. Not surprisingly, the guests are self-conscious and unsure how to interact with one another, and so they resort to taking pictures of the food, texting those who aren't there, and otherwise amusing themselves with their phones. Turkle says, "Here, phones provided a welcome alternative to talk" (141). But that alternative comes at a price:

> Before there were smartphones, an event such as the birthday party would have meant long silences, some stumbling around, and a few brief conversations with members of the opposite sex. These might have been awkward. But when they occurred, an important step would have been taken. Developmentally, the fifteen-year-olds would be closer to having sixteen-year-old confidence in their ability to connect. Eyes down at screen do not provide this groundwork. (141)

I suspect we can all remember an experience or two from adolescence that, though its memory may still make us cringe, did in fact teach us much about how to interact socially with others. Young people these days have far fewer opportunities for face-to-face interaction than did earlier generations. While young people were once active in social groups such as Scouts, 4-H, and church organizations, such groups seem outdated nowadays. Even clubs in school struggle to maintain an active membership. Traditional family gatherings have changed too, as instability in families increases and adults also find themselves swept up in the pull of technology. As one noteworthy finding from the Pew Research Center reveals, "About seven-in-ten parents say that their teen is distracted by their cellphone during conversations at least sometimes; half of teens say the same of their parents" (Jiang). So as traditional opportunities for positive social interactions disappear, our students desperately need some place where they can safely interact with one another and, in the process, learn the social skills necessary to navigate the larger world. The obvious place is the classroom—especially a classroom free of smartphones and screens.

As noted in the research, one of the reasons students prefer to use social media as a primary means of interaction is that it affords them time to think about what they want to say. Now, far be it from me or any other teacher to fault a teenager's desire to take the time to think, but there is another issue here. As we all know from IEPs and 504s and parent emails, many young people today suffer from anxiety: "According to the National Institutes of Health, nearly 1 in 3 of all adolescents ages 13–18 will experience an anxiety disorder" (C. McCarthy). For teenagers, social interactions are often highly stressful, as fear of judgment is strong. For many young people, the desire to pull back from face-to-face conversations is motivated by social anxiety. How much easier it is to engage only in "edited encounters." Turkle describes social media sites and texting as "where you share a self in process. But you share best if you can edit, because you want to share what your friends will find acceptable" (143). She goes on, "In interviews I conducted from 2008 to 2010 with high school and college students, they make it clear that the back-and-forth of unrehearsed 'real time' conversation is something that makes you 'unnecessarily' vulnerable" (143). Think about that. While adults might say "human," adolescents say "vulnerable." Perhaps if you could create a world where *all* human interaction took place virtually, this strategy for alleviating anxiety would be an effective one. But, fortunately, we don't live in such a world—yet, anyway. Our students will have to engage in face-to-face conversations in various situations as their world expands. They'll need to be interviewed by the boss at the fast-food restaurant where they want to work. They'll have to sit down with a college representative or alumnus. They'll one day likely want to do more than text-"talk" with a potential girl- or boyfriend and maybe even have an actual date. (And no matter how many times my students try to explain the rules of "talking" in the modern search for love, I just don't get it. Especially when they tell me they "talk" constantly over text with a prospective love interest who sits behind them in class but never say a word to that person in real life.) And maybe, just maybe, they'll want to sit and talk with other human beings, just to ease that existential loneliness that grows stronger as we grow older. The point is, unless one chooses to be a recluse, life involves actual conversation, or at least I hope it always will.

Conversation connects human beings—and it makes them happy. A 2018 study from the University of Arizona explored "substantial conversations," described by Matthias Mehl as "'conversations where real, meaningful information was exchanged[;] . . . it could be about any topic—politics, relationships, the weather—it just needs to be at a more than trivial level of depth'" (qtd. in Tsai). The study indicates that the quantity and quality of conversation one has have a direct impact on a person's happiness.

> First, quantity of conversations undeniably improves well-being. "The more conversations someone tended to have—that is, the more they were exposed to social interactions—the better they seemed to fare, and vice versa."
>
> Second, substantive conversations lead to a higher quality of life. Participants who had more substantive conversations with others reported a greater degree of happiness, overall. This was true both for extroverts and for introverts. (qtd. in Tsai).

We can encourage lifelong learning, but we should also consider how we can help our students to develop lifelong well-being. I worry that if students don't learn how to talk to one another, demonstrating interest and empathy, by the time they leave high school, they will find it difficult to ever develop those skills, and without them, life can be long and lonely.

The reflections my students wrote about conversation—both before and during the pandemic—indicate their awareness of the importance of conversation, even as they shy away from it. They further recognize how anxiety plays a major role in their inability to talk face to face. One writes, "My anxiety about communicating goes as far as emailing a teacher after class instead of asking them a quick question while I am sitting in their class. I think this also has to do with how we have all grown up. Most of us have grown up communicating through social media." Another says, "I obsess over the littlest things. In conversations this often makes me so panicky about saying the wrong or boring or stupid thing that I sometimes flat out lie to avoid judgment for how I think or for the things I like. . . . I lie in conversation because it's so much less scary than being honest."

I read these lines and wonder how we got here. We're talking about asking a question or expressing a preference. We're talking about human conversation, an ability that has defined us and advanced us as a species. We're talking about the primary means of human connection and our best hope for creating true community. Yet many of our young people panic at the mere idea of holding a conversation, even, as the following classroom situation shows, when that conversation has a technical component.

In the *Atlantic* article "My Students Don't Know How to Have a Conversation," teacher-writer Paul Barnwell describes what happens when he asks his high school juniors to create podcasts in small groups. As students of the digital age, podcasts are part of their vocabulary, and one would think this is something they could do with ease—and pleasure. But that's not the case:

> Even with plenty of practice, the task proved daunting to students. I watched trial runs of their podcasts frequently fall silent. Unless the student facilitator asked a question, most kids were unable to converse effectively. Instead of chiming in or following up on comments, they conducted rigid interviews. They shuffled papers and looked down at their hands. Some even reached for their phones—an automatic impulse and the last thing they should be doing. (Barnwell)

I think we've all seen this sort of behavior in our classrooms when students are working in small groups, presenting to the class, or even informally talking to each other. At times I've brushed it off as simple teenage awkwardness, but why then, I ask myself, after decades of teaching, am I finding my students' inability to converse such a problem in recent years—and why are my concerns shared by teachers and researchers alike?

I think we have to accept that we are dealing with a new breed of adolescent, one who has grown up in a world that is filled with technology and who has continued to adapt to it. That is not something we can undo, nor should we. Our students have exceptional skills when it comes to manipulating technology and using it to advance their learning. But the acquisition of one skill set should not mean the loss of another, especially one as important as human conversation.

Barnwell expresses concern that

> in our zealous rush to meet 21st century demands—emailing assignments, customizing projects for tablets and laptops, and allowing students to BYOD (Bring Your Own Device)—we aren't asking students to think and communicate in real time. Online discussion boards and Twitter are useful tools for exchanging ideas. But they often encourage a "read, reflect, forget about it" response that doesn't truly engage students in extended critical thinking or conversation.

In the process of researching for this book, I came across many online articles supporting the need for classroom conversation. Some, of course, were scholarly and informative, but a good many began by expounding on the importance of class discussion—and ended with an endorsement for some sort of technology-based "assistance" in promoting conversation. I believe we need to be wary of such advice. First, as Barnwell clearly explains, the overuse of technology in the classroom has contributed to the absence of conversation there. But beyond that, the conversational interactions students have on screen are different from those in real time, as I suspect any teacher who spent a good part of the pandemic engaged in remote learning can attest. As people experienced in orchestrating dialogue in our physical classrooms, we know there is a singular, what I call "staccato," movement to on-screen conversations that renders the exchange somewhat graceless and certainly altered, and students often fail to maintain focus in such situations. There is a good reason for this, as Daniel T. Willingham, professor of psychology at the University of Virginia, explains:

> A class discussion requires conversational turn-taking, and eye movements play a central role. For example, if you are speaking, and I break eye contact, that indicates I want a conversational turn. If I'm speaking, a prolonged gaze signals an intention to yield the floor.
>
> These signals are lost in videoconferencing, both because internet lag disrupts their timing and because computer equipment makes eye contact difficult. I see your eyes when I look at my screen, but you see my eyes when I look at my camera. The disconnect is part of why Zoom meetings brim with disruptions and awkward pauses.

Willingham goes on to discuss possible fixes for this disconnect, the most significant being the presence of "a facilitator (usually a parent)," noting that "companies that provide online education to home schoolers routinely stipulate that an adult supervise an elementary or middle school student."

But as facilitators of conversation in our classrooms, we need to do more than just supervise. Scientists and linguists can break down the dynamics of human conversation in ways that can help teachers understand some of the subtleties of classroom conversation and make us aware of the importance of our actions as we choreograph these interactions. In the 2020 Phi Delta Kappan article "Conversation in the Classroom," researchers Carrie Holmberg and Jamaal Muwwakkil discuss the complexities inherent in any classroom discussion:

> It may seem silly to state, but teachers have spent more time in a classroom than students have and, therefore, have had more time to become accustomed to the conventions of classroom conversation. Because students may have differing degrees of familiarity with the nuances of classroom discussion, their conversational behavior might not align with instructors' perceived norms. If educators become more aware of their own perceived norms, and subtle differences among students' ways of talking, they'll be better equipped to set clear expectations and validate the different ways students communicate. And the less educators know about these variations, the more likely they'll be to exclude and/or misunderstand some

> students, particularly so-called "quieter" students, those who are ever-so-slightly "slower" than their peers to process spoken language, English learners (ELs), and students (both ELs and non-ELs) with cultural communicative practices that do not align with the classroom culture. (Holmberg and Muwwakkil)

It may be impossible for a teacher to be attentive to all the specific dynamics involved when a classroom conversation is in full swing, but the simple awareness of conversational differences among students is essential, as is the teacher's willingness to work to ease these differences in order to make class conversation inclusive and positive for all students. Holmberg and Muwwakkil discuss a few strategies that many of us employ but perhaps have never really considered the deeper implications of. For example, the Think-Pair-Share technique often used to get all students involved in conversation offers an important opportunity for "rehearsal" for English learners. Another strategy the authors suggest: "To better balance participation in small-group discussions, students can hold equal numbers of participation chips, giving up one chip per conversational turn." Although I've used a similar technique myself (see Chapter 8, "Tricks of the Trade,"), I had never thought about how it's connected to turn-taking and the way our students interreact with one another. A third idea emphasizes the impact of physical space: "For more softly spoken students, the teacher's physical positioning in the room can help tremendously: Moving diagonally opposite the speaker so the student needs to project to be heard can work" (Holmberg and Muwwakkil).

The essential point is that human conversation, as innate as it may be, isn't the same for all individuals, and as teachers we need to be aware of how different our students are in their conversational abilities and styles. Holmberg and Muwwakkil caution teachers not to simply dismiss a student as soft-spoken or quiet but rather to recognize that many factors come into play as a young person develops a conversational style. So much is dependent on a person's background, upbringing, and personal experience—and I would also include one's level of involvement with technology. I think sometimes of peers in my youth who were looked at oddly because their parents raised them with no TV, and I suspect they may have been more interesting, articulate students than the rest of us. Perhaps too those students today whose access to technology has been limited by parental choice and replaced with other means of experiencing the world have different ways of navigating the classroom and connecting to those within it.

Another area of research relevant to the topic of classroom conversation that is important for educators to consider concerns how well we do—or do not—

prepare our students for their future. A 2006 study conducted by Peter D. Hart Research Associates Inc. for the Association of American Colleges and Universities presented the following finding:

> One area of particular concern to most business executives is that they perceive many recent college graduates to have poor written and oral communications skills. Indeed, they feel that today's graduates have weaker communications skills than did previous generations. Some participants blame this decline on young people's increased reliance on e-mail, instant messaging, and text messaging. A few recognize that many students fall behind in their communications skills before they even enter college, forcing colleges and universities to focus on remedial instruction in this area. (Peter D. Hart Research Associates)

Yet more than a decade later, similar research by Hart Research Associates reveals that we have done little to remediate the situation. As Ken Lindblom and Leila Christenbury note in *Continuing the Journey 3*, "A 2018 survey of business executives and hiring mangers listed 'able to effectively communicate orally' as the highest learning priority among this group and cut across majors (Association of American Colleges & Universities)" (55). Yet "only 40% of executives and 47% of hiring managers rate recent college graduates as well prepared in this area" ("Fulfilling the American Dream").

I think as teachers we have to consider our accountability in this situation. Yes, society has changed, and educators and business professionals may be justified in placing blame on the tools of technology that have changed the way we all communicate with one another. But the simple fact is, these changes are here to stay—as is the need for effective oral communication both in the workplace and beyond. As high school teachers, we have both the responsibility and the *ability* to potentially rectify this problem.

A September 2018 article in *Education Week*, "Speaking Skills Top Employer Wish Lists. But Schools Don't Teach Them," by Catherine Gewertz left me feeling a bit ashamed of our profession. She contends that reading and writing are the primary focus of the English classroom primarily because those are the skills addressed in mandated state testing programs. Despite the fact that the Common Core State Standards include speaking and listening standards, those skills are not generally included in the actual tests, and so teachers fail to give these skills the time they deserve in the classroom. We often rail against the limitations of standardized tests, decrying their inability to recognize creativity and individual learning styles, but this is another concern we need to consider—that we allow anything not "on the test" to be relegated to a backseat in our classrooms.

Second, Gewertz notes that the communication skills we *do* teach in school aren't necessarily the ones that translate to the workplace. She lists activities such as class presentations and debates, seeing a "mismatch" with the oral communication skills that employers seek—and rarely find. Among these skills are:

- Constructing a clear, concise message and tailoring it to different audiences
- Interacting well with a team (discussing ideas respectfully with colleagues, formulating good questions, being prepared for thorough answers)
- Participating respectfully in conversations to resolve conflict (Gewertz)

This list encapsulates what most of us would simply call *talk*—that give and take between people who want to connect well with one another. It's what we do when we come together with a desire to share thoughts and ideas and with a willingness to learn from one another. It involves openness, intelligence, and courtesy—and it is what makes us human. Yet it's missing from many of our classrooms and from our students' lives.

The *Education Week* article ends with a line that may or may not be pointed. I choose to read it as the former. In an effort to inspire cooperation between business and education in order to improve students' communication skills, Caitlin Codella, senior director of the US Chamber of Commerce Foundation Center for Education and Workforce, says this: "'Schools can't understand the skills employers need without having a conversation with employers'" (qtd. in Gewertz). Can we understand anything about each other without conversation? I don't think so. And that is the problem.

II

Toward a Solution

It is the province of knowledge to speak and it is the privilege of wisdom to listen.
—*Oliver Wendell Holmes*

I would be arrogant, if not daft, to suggest that I have the solution for the problems our students face as they struggle to communicate face to face with one another and with the wider world. We are living in a world where change is inevitable, and there is no going backward. Technology will continue to surprise us with all it can do, and we should neither expect nor hope for young people to turn away from it. There will continue to be political and social divides that feel too vast to cross, and there will be crises and challenges that shake us as a country and as a people. Amidst all this, we may grow more distant from one another. And we are fooling ourselves if we think our students are not aware of all this. Consider one student's words:

> Conversations in and out of school don't occur as much as they used to, as if we're starting to forget how to talk. People's minds are being trapped in a differentiated world, the Internet, creating a distraction from the interaction between people. It is zoning people into videos and games, which people would rather use than talk. It is creating barriers and bubbles, blocking people from others. And the people hiding within the barriers are too afraid to break them down and open up. Generations are coming for which screens and devices are a necessity and something for constant use.

> Society today is separated into groups, and it's as if only the people in these groups can talk with one another. And as a society we are becoming very sensitive to certain topics and offended by the slightest bit. . . . We isolate ourselves from each other when the best solution could be talking it out and growing tougher skins.

I may be exaggerating to call this a cry for help—but maybe not. I think our students are hungry for genuine human connection, and I think it has become our responsibility as teachers to help them find it. Though these days we are asked to do more in our classrooms than we possibly can, the truth is, some things matter more than others—and one of those things is human connection found through authentic conversation. As Ralph Ellison said, "Education is all a matter of building bridges." What builds bridges, connections, and links between human beings better than the words we speak to one another?

I hope you will find in the following chapters the reasons to incorporate more conversation in your classroom and the practical suggestions and strategies to make that happen. Conversation is not something we have to *add* to our lengthy list of classroom activities; it is something we can successfully *integrate* with all that we already do. Our classrooms are small communities of individuals who have much in common but who also possess unique qualities, beliefs, and experiences they can share with one another to the benefit of all. Each classroom is, in a sense, a microcosm of society, and if in that space students can learn to stand up and speak, sit back and listen, and intelligently process and act on all that they hear, they can grow both as individuals and as citizens of society. There is a wonderful line by Robert Frost: "Education is the ability to listen to almost anything without losing your temper or your self-confidence." I think how different the world would be today if we could all claim that ability, and I think that we as educators would be wise to make that a goal for all of our students—and perhaps for ourselves.

So, while I have no absolute solutions to ease the disconnection or detachment that characterizes too many of our students, I do have faith in teachers and our ability to build bridges that can join them to one another and to us. I hope that in the pages that follow you will find exactly what you need in order to encourage connection and conversation among all our students before, as the young writer above fears, it is too late and we do forget how to talk.

"What Do You Have to Say for Yourself?"

The art of conversation is the art of hearing as well as of being heard.

—*William Hazlitt*

Often, when a class discussion wobbles and my students seem particularly reluctant to speak, I berate myself. Occasionally, but only in my head, I berate them. Sometimes I stop the faltering discussion to ask them what's going on and why no one is participating, and there are times when they tell me. But no one has ever told me quite as explicitly as Danielle all that goes on in a student's mind as her hand wavers between desk and air.

One of my favorite writing activities is one I first borrowed years ago from Dan Kirby, Dawn Kirby and Tom Liner. Described in *Inside Out: Strategies for Teaching Writing*, the Talking Back to Yourself exercise challenges students to write a dialogue in which two sides of their own voice argue with each other (83–85). It's an excellent way of getting students to write in a voice that is real and their own. When my students tackle this assignment, I always give them the freedom to choose a situation that is authentic and significant for them. I tell them to think of a dilemma they have experienced, the kind of situation that makes them feel tugged in two directions. It might be an issue of saving money or spending it on a new video game, getting a summer job or taking one last summer of freedom, or, as Danielle surprised me with, deciding to speak in class or remaining silent.

Danielle titled her piece "3 Seconds." She is the first of my students to write about the moment when a student debates whether to raise their hand to participate in class discussion. When I first read the piece, I immediately appreciated its originality. But when I read it again, I was struck by how fraught the decision is to raise one's voice in class discussion, and by how much we ask of students when we urge them to enter a conversation.

Danielle's seemingly simple and straightforward dialogue, with each side of her brain reacting to and responding to the other, revealed all that can happen in a student's mind in a mere three seconds (or maybe a little more). While I gaze out at my students, anticipating the pleasure this discussion will produce, they are apparently waging internal warfare:

> Hmm, I think I could add something to this conversation about the reading. I'm gonna raise my hand.
>
> No.
>
> What?
>
> NO. Don't raise your hand.
>
> Why not?
>
> Because the teacher won't call on you. There are sooo many other people in the class who are smarter than you that are going to be called on.
>
> So what? Dumb people talk all the time, sometimes incessantly.
>
> Yes, but that's another reason you shouldn't. Don't follow the societal norms of stupidity!
>
> Hey, you don't have to be so mean to me! Let's just go back to civil argument.
>
> You're right, of course. I apologize.
>
> Thank you. Sooo . . . why shouldn't I raise my hand?
>
> Because she'll call on someone else! She can't even see your hand over the person in front of you!
>
> Well, I'll raise my hand even higher.
>
> You can't do that! That just makes it seem like you're trying too hard to be noticed.
>
> Okay, so I won't do that. I'll just hope she sees me!
>
> You can do that, and MAYBE she'll call on you, but what will you say?
>
> I can touch upon what the last person said.
>
> But it's been so long since they started their point, you've probably already forgotten what you were gonna say!
>
> No, I remember!
>
> Then what is it?
>
> . . . um
>
> My point exactly.
>
> But . . . I . . . I could . . . I could bring up something completely new.
>
> Isn't that the slightest bit awkward though? Just transitioning from one topic to a completely new one? What if people have something to say about the current topic, and you cut them off? They wouldn't be very happy with you.
>
> You're right . . . they wouldn't. . . .

> Now look, the class has already started on a new topic!
>
> Really? I guess it's pointless to raise my hand now....

As I read that last line, *I guess it's pointless to raise my hand now . . .* , I wondered just how many times Danielle had missed her opportunity to talk and how many times I had failed to notice that she had something to say.

In a reflection, written after Danielle had completed her final draft, she explained what she hoped she had achieved in the dialogue: "The two sides represent the optimist and the realist in people. One side wants to share their ideas with the class and participate in the conversation, and the other side knows that it's a bad idea to speak when there are other people in the conversation who are smarter and know more about the topic than I do." I had to read that sentence twice to realize—or maybe to *accept*—that, for students, the idea of successfully participating in class discussion seems wildly optimistic, and that for many of them, their reality is that they won't measure up and are better off keeping quiet.

The concerns Danielle describes are clearly ones that impact conversation in all our classrooms, and they are issues we as teachers need to both recognize and address. One category of her concerns can be easily addressed by the teacher, and that is a student's ability to be noticed by the teacher and invited into the discussion. Then, once students are in the conversation, the teacher needs to step back to give them responsibility for steering it. This is part of the discussion design.

As Danielle points out, one of the things that deters students from speaking in class is their inability to be heard—or sometimes even seen. As she says, there are "sooo many people" in a classroom, and the teacher has only one set of eyes. Certain students are vigorous hand raisers, and they are always noticed. Then there are those students who dispense with hand raising entirely and simply call out their responses; even when we attempt to quiet them, somehow they always do make themselves heard. Yet other students, as the diffident side of Danielle demonstrates, are tentative. Their eyes may tell you that they want to be heard, but their hands remain on their desks and they don't speak up. As teachers it's our job to be proactive, to "hear" what isn't being said, but that isn't easy.

One of my most positive teaching experiences involved team teaching. Beyond the many obvious benefits of having two teachers in one classroom, the best part was that, while my colleague was speaking, I could read our students' faces. I could usually tell who was confused, who wanted to speak, and who had tuned out completely. With only one teacher in the classroom, the task becomes much more difficult, and it's almost impossible to balance the attention you give to the material with the attention you give to each individual student.

But facilitating a class discussion means more than keeping the conversation moving, asking probing questions, and clarifying confusing ideas. It also means circulating through the room, watching the group, seeing whose head nods, whose hand teeters in the air, whose face says, "I *think* I want to say something." While I'm not a proponent of cold calling and respect a student's right to remain silent, I never want a student to feel that they are drowned out by other voices in the room. If I can encourage a student with a line like, "Danielle, you're kind of looking like you want to say something?," then that is what I need to say. Such words open the door for a student to speak, for if they have to wait too long to interject a comment or idea, they often lose motivation or nerve, or even, as Danielle points out, forget what they have to say. At the same time, my students understand that, when I do open this metaphorical door, they don't have to go through. When I say, "Did you want to add something?," a student can simply say, "No," and the discussion moves on.

In many ways, a teacher leading a discussion is like a conductor leading an orchestra. Just as a good conductor knows the score *and* the musicians, so too does a good teacher know the material and the students. Just as a conductor realizes that every single instrument contributes to the success of the piece, so too does a teacher know that the voices of all students, when heard in harmony, will create a particular kind of music. It doesn't happen naturally, but it should *appear* as though it does.

In "What Does a Conductor Actually Do?," Clemency Burton-Hill quotes Tom Service, author of *Music as Alchemy: Journeys with Great Conductors and Their Orchestras*, as saying, "'The best conductors are the best listeners. They become a lightning rod of listening; a focus so that the players and the conductor can become something bigger than all of them—than all of us—at the same time as feeling fully realised as individuals'" (qtd. in Burton-Hill).

Teaching too is alchemy, and discussion perhaps the best example of it. When a classroom full of students is actively engaged in discussion, magic happens and hearts and minds are transformed. At the helm is the teacher, who should be the "lightening rod of listening"—but that role as listener is one we teachers sometimes find hard to adopt. For a good discussion to occur, we need to lead by listening, but that is counter to much of our training. We're taught to be in charge, and even the most nonauthoritarian teacher typically feels responsible for the activity within their classroom. So, in preparation for a class discussion, we compile specific questions that get at critical aspects of the material, we organize them in a logical sequence, and we strategize about how to best present each idea. With this battle plan in hand and our students before us, we initiate the discussion, ready to move it along at a steady pace. But in the process, we all too often fail to listen. We fail to hear what it is that our students care about and what they *need* to discuss in order to feel invested in the material and to fully understand it.

I think of a "discussion" my juniors and seniors had about August Wilson's play *Fences*. I went into the discussion wanting them to understand Troy's relationship with his son Cory and to realize that, despite his seemingly cold-hearted behavior when he tells his son, "'Liked you? Who the hell say I got to like you?'" (37), he is fulfilling what he sees as his role as a father. In this pivotal scene between Troy and Cory, Troy proceeds to defend his role as a father by listing all he has done for his son, providing him with food, shelter, and clothing. In my mind, it was important for my students to understand that, based on the time period and on Troy's own background as a son who had been abandoned by his mother and left with a harsh father who nonetheless stayed and raised Troy and his ten siblings, Troy lived up to what he believed was his responsibility as a father. My students, however, couldn't grasp that idea and simply despised Troy.

"But it was a different time," I reasoned. "It was 1959 and life was so difficult for African American families. For Troy to give his son food, shelter, clothing, that was a big deal."

"But he blocks all Cory's chances. He won't let him be recruited for football. He just wants him to work at the A&P all his life," a student countered.

In my defense, I will say I looked hopefully around the room to see if anyone wanted to help me champion Troy and to suggest that maybe he just wanted his son to have a stable future, but it seemed they were all glaring at me.

"He's just jealous of Cory," one boy announced, and there was a general murmur of agreement.

"But Troy believes he didn't make it in the major leagues because he was Black," I said. "Maybe he's trying to protect his son from that sort of discrimination—and disappointment."

A few laugh derisively.

"Nah, he's just a jerk." This from the same boy. "He doesn't want his kid to be better than him. And he tells Cory he doesn't even like him."

"Does he actually say that?" I ask. "Let's look back at the text. Troy says, 'Who the hell say I got to like you? What law is there say I got to like you?.' Is he possibly saying that his primary responsibility as a father is something different?"

And so I kept pushing, *explaining* what I believed Wilson wanted them to understand about Troy, until my own refusal to listen to what my students were saying pretty much ended the discussion—if you can call me versus them "discussion."

A classroom discussion has to be more than the teacher squaring off against the students. It's important for a teacher to have goals for a discussion, and I would have been remiss had I not wanted students to see Troy from different angles. But that's my agenda, not my students', and in a true discussion—not a debate—they should come to discover various sides of the issue through the process of conversation. They should walk out of class, ideas whirling in their heads, not annoyed by the teacher's insistence or feeling they were wrong.

The next year I remembered this less than successful classroom "discussion" and decided to approach the father-son relationship differently. I began by asking my students to individually jot down qualities they felt a good father should possess. I suggested they think of it as a sort of job description. After a few minutes, I put the opener *A good father should . . .* on the board and asked students to complete the sentence, which they did readily.

A good father should:

1. provide for his kids financially
2. always trust his kids
3. spend time with his kids/do stuff with them
4. love his kids no matter what
5. be a good role model
6. support his kids/be there when his kids need him
7. be strict with his kids when they need it
8. put his kids before himself

Once we had this list on the board, I asked students to think about what each saw as the top three qualifications for a good father, in order of importance. Then I opened up the class for discussion.

This became real discussion, conversation about the role of a father, one that I'm certain was influenced by the students' own relationships—or lack thereof—with their fathers, as well as by their experiences in the world. I noted with interest that there was a small cohort of students who firmly believed that a father's primary responsibility was to provide the basics for his children—food, clothing, and shelter.

As this discussion started to wind down, I saw the perfect opening to segue into a conversation about Troy's relationship with his son, and at that point I felt comfortable stepping back to allow my students to consider, on their own, Troy's rating on the father scale. This approach didn't diminish their animosity toward Troy when it came to his inability to see affection as central to the father-son relationship, and I completely respected the passion with which they attacked Troy. But conducting the discussion in this way, allowing them to consider their own personal views of fatherhood, did allow students to see Troy in a broader context and to escape a sort of tunnel vision mentality. Now too those students who did see financial support as a key aspect of a father's role could, on some level, defend Troy, rather than I, as the teacher, telling the class what to think.

What does this mean in terms of the design of a discussion? What it first and foremost means is that the teacher has to find a way to put the discussion in the hands of the students. In *Discussion as a Way of Teaching*, Brookfield and Preskill explain,

> In general, reticence on the part of the discussion leader is a virtue. The leader's contribution can interrupt the momentum of a stimulating exchange or get in the way of a student who is speaking up for the first time. It can also effectively steal the spotlight away from a student who has worked through some difficult ideas. If the teacher is an active but relatively nonverbal participant, the discussion can become focused on the ideas of the students and their struggle to make meaning. This goal is almost certainly more valuable than whatever the teacher might want to say. (200)

It is appropriate for the teacher to have goals for the discussion in order to ensure that students address important aspects of the literature or the topic being discussed, but those goals should not impose such a rigid structure on the discussion that students have no space to explore. Just as most of us eschew conversation with those who "take charge" and control the exchange for their own purposes, so too do students lose interest in discussion that seems destined to promote only the teacher's views. In our planning, then, we need to think not only about the key points we want to cover, but equally as much about how to create an atmosphere that will allow as many students as possible to find their way to those significant ideas in the most natural way possible. I was wrong to open the discussion by asking my students what they thought of the relationship between Troy and Cory. The intensity of *Fences* makes the reader automatically feel animosity toward Troy, and students, who come to literature without all the worldly experience and knowledge of adult readers, need the time and space to consider what is beneath their immediate reactions if they are to see other perspectives. So now we don't start the discussion with Troy, whose very name seems to inflame these adolescent readers. Instead, we start with a conversation about fathers in general, which allows students to see Troy against that broader framework.

As a general suggestion, then, I would say that, in preparation for a discussion, the teacher needs to be cognizant of students' tendency to all too quickly align themselves with one side of an issue, perhaps because they are young and passionate and just learning to give voice to their beliefs, or sometimes because they simply misunderstand the material. But if we want them to talk—and listen to one another—we need to give them the power to steer the conversation. We need to find a way to put the discussion in their hands. And that is best achieved when we give them an "in" to the material. Should we expect students, in one reading, to fully understand the dynamics of Troy and Cory's complex relationship? No. But can we expect them to understand the role of fathers in general? Yes, and so that becomes the invitation to a student-centered discussion, and one in which the teacher steps back, is quiet, and lets the "music" begin.

I often used to open a discussion by asking my students a general question such as, "So what did you think of the story?" To me, that's an open invitation to talk about almost any aspect of the literature, and it's the kind of question someone in my adult book group would ask when we get down to talking about the book. From my perspective, it's a way of welcoming students into a conversation about the literature and a way of moving ourselves toward key aspects of the work. But my students are not book group devotees, and I have learned that to them it seems a trick question and often ends up being a roadblock to any real discussion. Typically, most of them stare at me blankly, unsure of what I'm really asking them, and perhaps hesitant to state their honest opinions. Once in a while, a bold student will say, "I hated it. It was boring," or sometimes, on a more positive note, another will say, "I loved it," and, when pressed, will follow up with a reason or two. But for most students, that "welcoming" question falls flat, and it's partly because that is not the question my students would ask.

Questioning is critical to learning—as well as to maintaining meaningful conversations. At the heart of both is a sense of curiosity, a desire to know more. In "The Right Questions," authors Dan Rothstein and Luz Santana explain the benefits of questioning:

> Question formulation promotes student voice and critical thinking. As students learn to produce their own questions, they are thinking *divergently*—that is, more broadly and creatively. When they focus on the kinds of questions they are asking and choose their priority questions, they are thinking *convergently*—narrowing down, analyzing, assessing, comparing, and synthesizing. And when they reflect on what they have learned through the process, students are engaged in *metacognition*—they are thinking about their thinking.

But when we as teachers rob students of the opportunity to *create their own questions* about the topic we are discussing, we deny them the chance to engage in these essential thinking processes, and we cut off potential for conversation that explores these questions.

To get authentic discussion started, it's far more effective to begin by asking students what *they* want to talk about. Sometimes they're bubbling over with questions and ideas. We read Mary Robison's "An Amateur's Guide to the Night," and they are desperate to know if the mother really has a brain tumor, or if she is delusional, or if she is simply a bad parent. They want to know if the absent father really did send Lindy a graduation card, and they are eager to discuss why the family is obsessed with all those horror movies. And Lindy and her mom double dating? What's that about? As they raise these questions and ideas, I write them on the board, feeling optimistic that students will soon be involved in a productive conversation about family dynamics and Robison's characters. But not all the literature we ask students to read is as immediately engaging for them as Robison's story, and there are many times when I ask what they want to talk about and they are silent.

When that happens, I take a few minutes of class time to ask each student to write down the questions, ideas, and opinions they have after reading the story that they would like the class to discuss. I suggest they thumb through the pages of the story to recall things they were curious about, puzzled by, or interested in. If students keep reading journals, this is a perfect opportunity for them to review their entries to remind themselves of what they felt mattered in the work. Once students have had time to compose a short list of topics, we then share them on the board. If, as is occasionally the case, students are still reluctant to verbally share their questions and ideas, I ask each to choose one entry from their list to put on a slip of paper and deposit in a "question box" on my desk. Then I draw out those pieces of paper and use them as discussion starters.

I've also utilized Rothstein and Santana's four-step process called the Question Formulation Technique. This technique is particularly effective in those classes and situations where students struggle to even begin to formulate questions, as it frees them from thinking they have to ask the "right" questions.

- Ask as many questions as you can.
- Do not stop to judge, discuss, edit, or answer any question.
- Write down every question exactly as it was asked.
- Change any statements into questions. (Rothstein and Santana)

I have found, though, that generally students do ask the "right" questions; that is, they are aware of and interested in the most significant aspects of the story, and the things they want to discuss are usually many of the same things I have gathered in my own notes. If I open the door wide to discussion, they will most likely touch on the same ideas I would have presented had I taken charge of the discussion in my own way. But, and it *is* a big but, the conversation is not going to be as well organized or as logical as I might like. That, however, is something I have to accept if I want to engage more students in genuine discussion. The conversation my students have based on the questions, phrases, and ideas on the board may play out a bit like a pinball game, caroming from one idea to the next, without us ever fully wrapping up or resolving an idea or concept—and that may make me crazy. But that's what actual conversation does; it roams and rambles, all the while engaging the participants who are invested in it.

I think back to the book group model. I know some book groups are run like many classrooms, with a leader in charge and a clear-cut structure that outlines how participants can share their ideas. I tried one of those book groups once years ago, and not only did I not enjoy the group, but I quickly lost interest in the book we were discussing. Even as an English teacher and avid reader, I felt almost intimidated, as if every idea I offered ought to be polished and perfect and "correct." I remember thinking that it reminded me of "School"—and I wonder now why I didn't make the connection to my students and their own struggles with discussion. In the book group I delight in now, conversation is relaxed, unstructured, and exuberant, and we frequently interrupt each other with ideas that tumble over one another. It is, I know, not considered the perfect model for a class discussion, but the enthusiasm and the joy we experience is something I want to replicate in my classroom, and I believe that comes from discussion that arises from within the participants. When I let my students begin a discussion with what interests them, as with the compelling question of what is wrong with Lindy's mother, I know they will run with it. And if in their eagerness to discuss many aspects of the story they fail to resolve certain issues, I can always go back to recap the conversation later, clarifying confusing points and emphasizing key ideas they should remember. As for resolution, what does that mean in terms of literature anyway, and are we, as teachers, perhaps doing a disservice to literature when we attempt to "wrap it up" and explain what it all means?

Discussion design, then, is very much in the teacher's purview, and that design can definitely affect the quality and quantity of student participation. But as teachers, we cannot completely erase a second major deterrent to successful discussion, and that is students' fear. They fear failure, they fear judgment, and they fear giving offense. Some even fear the simple act of speaking. Some of this fear I discuss in Chapter 1, but I want to look more closely here at the fear of judgment and to offer some suggestions for counteracting it with some specific classroom strategies and activities.

The fear of judgment weighs heavily on students, and it happens even when a student feels confident in their views. It takes a lot to be the outlier, especially in adolescence. Though some students seem to thrive on being contrary, most are happiest as part of the pack. So, when your peers are passionately attacking Troy for his lack of paternal instinct and you believe he is doing his best as a father, how likely are you to speak your mind? As noted in Chapter 1, in their written reflections on conversation in the classroom, students repeatedly echo this sort of comment: "I feel I don't talk much in class anymore due to how judged I feel when I speak my mind."

Judgment is a word with which adolescents are all too familiar. The same pressure they feel on social media affects them in a classroom of peers, and they are well aware of the sharp divides in our society and how easy it is to be labeled this or that, based on even just one opinion. Students have learned to be cautious in expressing their views, and while such circumspection and sensitivity to the views of others is laudable, it's distressing to find students withholding views for fear of judgment. This creates anxiety that impacts their willingness to speak in class. As another student writes, "I'm always afraid people will think what I say is stupid." How many of our students feel the same and so feign agreement with the majority to avoid seeming stupid or wrong, even when they hold dissenting views and valid reasons to support them? When students are hesitant to speak because of a fear of judgment, they are robbed of their voice, and that is tragic. Beyond that, however, the class as a whole is robbed of the opportunity to see issues from varying perspectives and, introduced to new information, to perhaps rethink their own views. As one student says eloquently in a reflection, "Sometimes, someone bringing up a point in class or talking out ideas with someone will bring out thoughts you didn't know you had until they just came out. If you're feeling stuck, sometimes one small thing someone says in a conversation can spark another train of ideas that you weren't able to find in your brain before." Isn't that what we're always trying to do—to help students "find in their brain" new ideas and thoughts? Of course, the teacher can always be the proponent of an unpopular view, such as that of Troy being a good father, but students are often more open to such an idea if it comes from a classmate. The teacher's task, then, is to find a way to encourage that singular thinker to speak.

One of my favorite ways to promote discussion that welcomes opposing views is to ask, "Will someone please play devil's advocate? Will someone, whether you believe it or not, offer an opposing view with some reasons to support it?" This challenge generally stirs up those students who like to disagree just as a matter of course, but more important, it allows those students who might actually hold a less than popular view to express it, without ownership and an immediate fear of judgment. At first, they're just playing the devil's advocate game, but often, as the discussion continues, they find others coming to their side, and they realize they have the ability to turn a minority opinion into one that has strong appeal. At the same time, other students realize the importance of listening to opposing views without judgment, and they discover that sometimes what they hear affects their own views. And isn't that what real conversation does? It allows each of us, through the interplay of ideas, to strengthen or to reassess what we believe. As I'm always telling my students, there is no shame in changing one's mind.

Sometimes, to offer students a visual demonstration of how conversation can affect a person's perspective, I'll direct them, as they begin to express views on a topic, to stand in a certain section of the room. So those who believe Lindy's mother is actually suffering from a brain tumor all move to the corner by the windows. Those who think she is mentally unstable stand near the door. Those who see her simply as a bad parent find a spot in the front of the room. And those who are conflicted and unsure hover in the middle. If there are students who have completely different interpretations, I point them to other areas in the room. Then we start talking. This isn't a debate, I tell them. It's a conversation, just like we would have if they were all sitting in their seats, only now they are physically in a space that delineates their beliefs. This activity is also helpful in getting all students to commit to a belief and to participate, at least in the choice of a physical space, in the discussion.

As the conversation continues and students begin to hear new ideas, I encourage them to move about the room and to join whatever group they feel most strongly aligned with, depending on what they have heard. Some students stand their ground and never budge, but it's not uncommon for other students to move once or twice and back and forth. Those who were in the middle almost always hear something that makes them decide to join a group, and occasionally those with unique ideas find themselves with a new band of supporters. Besides the fact that students like the simple act of moving—and like seeing immediately how their comments and opinions impact listeners—this activity allows them to realize that there is nothing wrong with changing one's mind, and that we might sometimes be wise to do so. I quote Ralph Waldo Emerson's famous line from "Self-Reliance"—"A foolish consistency is the hobgoblin of little minds" (153)—because I want them to understand that there is nothing weak or wishy-washy about changing one's opinion. It is, in fact, a sign of intelligence to continually reassess one's ideas based on additional information. I also remind them that one's willingness to rethink a belief or position indicates an open mind and the ability to see more than one side. That, for me, is a major goal of all conversation in my classroom—to increase tolerance and understanding among individuals.

To that end, it's important, of course, that the teacher makes it a priority to establish a classroom where tolerance is a fundamental principle. At the start of a school year, I don't hand out any written classroom rules to my students but this one: *Be nice to each other.* And when I talk about this, I'm more serious in my demeanor than I am at almost any other time. I need my students to know from the very beginning that my classroom is a space where everyone's ideas are welcome. Certainly this philosophy is tested in specific situations, but from the beginning I need students to understand that I, as their teacher, am committed to making the space we share a judgment-free zone. I don't hesitate to share my own opinions with them, but, as I explain in Chapter 1, I continue to reiterate to them that my views in no way impact my feelings toward them as individuals, nor do they impact my assessment of their work. More than once, my often liberal views have put me in conflict with those of a conservative student, but it is the views that are in conflict, not us as people. In fact, I tell my students, I *need* them to express opposing views if we are ever to have any truly fruitful discussion in class. It's vital that, as the teacher, I consistently model an open and accepting attitude if I expect my students to do so. We can—and should—disagree, but that must not affect the human connection we have.

None of this completely settles a student's fear of judgment when it comes to joining in classroom conversation. But it's my responsibility to work to alleviate that fear, both through techniques and classroom activities and through my own attitude and words. When a student offers an unpopular view or one that seems somewhat "out there," I'm careful to take them seriously, to ask the same sort of clarifying questions I would ask a student who offered a more accepted view, and to demonstrate my own careful consideration of their ideas. I'm careful not to fawn over that student's comments or to feign support I don't feel, but I am sincere in expressing appreciation of their willingness to offer another viewpoint. I think students appreciate this, and whether intentionally or not, they often adopt the behavior they see modeled.

There are times, though, when students are not so malleable, when one or two dominate and in effect shut down the discussion in a class. In extreme situations, I've decided to confront this head-on by speaking privately to these students, but generally I'm loath to make this a teacher-student issue when, in fact, it's a class concern. So, when I see class discussion faltering time and time again because of class dynamics, I tell students that I'm honestly concerned about the quality of class discussion and that I'd like each to freewrite anonymously about how they view the discussions we've been attempting and how they might suggest we improve the discussion process. I emphasize that I'd like each of them to also consider what they might do differently to make our discussions go better. I don't want finger-pointing in these papers. I don't want to know who personally feels what about whom. I simply want students to reflect on what's going on with us as a group and to think about their own responsibility to the group and how each could help to improve our interactions.

When I read through these pieces, I take notes on what is said, particularly what is said repeatedly. When I share with my students the concerns and suggestions they have expressed, I do so in a way that I hope is neither pointed nor condemning. I'm not trying to single out the "bullies"—nor the students who contribute virtually nothing to the discussions. What I'm trying to do is make students see that a class discussion is a group effort and that each individual has a responsibility to the group if there is to be a positive outcome. I tell them what *I* intend to do to help facilitate better discussion, I offer them examples from the freewrites of things their peers have promised to do, and I remind them that I'm counting on all of them to make these individual changes for the good of the group.

If nothing else, this activity proves to students just how seriously I take class discussion. It's not a Friday afternoon filler or an end-of-the-period afterthought. It is central to my teaching and their learning, and we are all in it together. The chemistry of a class may mean that discussion is stilted or difficult, but, as with any human interaction, that can be changed through each individual's effort. It doesn't just happen; it demands intentional action on the part of each of us. And that interpersonal work is a lesson in itself, a lesson that will affect my students throughout their lives.

Though fear of judgment is certainly a powerful force, I've seen many students hesitate to participate in even in the most friendly and supportive classroom situations. In these cases, it can seem less because of a particular fear than an overall lack of confidence. It can of course be difficult to determine whether a student is quiet due to a lack of confidence or simply because that's their nature. Some students are just more introverted than others. They are more comfortable as observers rather than as participants, and I think a teacher needs to respect that. Often on Parents' Night, I'll ask a parent of a very reserved student if their son or daughter is quiet at home, and frequently the answer is yes, that the individual has always been quiet. That student may then be perfectly content hovering on the edges of a class discussion, and it may not serve any positive purpose for me to push them into the fray. But it's a different case with a student who seems shy only in a particular classroom situation, perhaps because they don't know the other students well, or perhaps they aren't confident in their abilities as an English student, or perhaps the structure of a large group intimidates them. Or, as often happens these days, perhaps they're the product of an educational culture that has convinced them there is one right answer, and they believe they don't have it, while others definitely do. As one student writes, "In class discussion, a couple people dominate, and the others don't speak up. I'm always nervous to speak up because I'm afraid I'll be wrong, but the people who dominate always are correct." As a teacher, I find it's a delicate decision to determine whether to push a student who seems to lack confidence or to let them languish, and I admit, in an attempt to alleviate pressure on such students, I may too often err on the side of the latter.

The truth of this was brought home to me during the period of remote learning. Though it seemed most of my students suffered from the lack of human interaction and, as a result, produced work that grew steadily more mediocre in quality, a few seemed to thrive in the relative isolation of computer-based learning. Though these students had been very quiet in class, their emails to me were often chatty and effusive, and their work showed a newfound confidence and a sort of daring, including a willingness to take chances with assignments and go beyond what was required.

Nowhere did I see this more than in Olivia's work. An Honors student, she had always done well in terms of her written work, but she seemed almost resolutely quiet in class and only rarely ventured an opinion or idea. Had the school year gone as it usually does, she likely would have earned an A but disappeared quickly from my mind. As it turned out after weeks of remote learning, I don't think I will ever forget Olivia, or what she taught me.

As one of their assignments during the quarantine, I asked students to choose a favorite poem to share both with me and with one or two others of their choice. I asked them to engage in an actual conversation (by phone or with someone in their home) about the poem, and then to "talk" with me over email about the poem and the reactions it evoked. Olivia chose a poem by rupi kaur from the collection *milk and honey*. It's a poem about blooming, and ends with the lines, "however you need / just bloom". In her email, Olivia wrote,

> For me, "blooming" has always been difficult. I feel like to bloom is to share yourself with others, and that's not something I have always found to be easy. I am a quiet person, and the idea of "blooming," especially when I was younger, seemed daunting. Nevertheless, it always felt like others were doing it so easily, and it was frustrating. But this poem reminds me that we are all different, and we will not all "bloom" the same way. As long as I'm doing it, little by little, I am doing it right, just like everyone else is.

These poignant lines reminded me that our students are not automatons, programmed to behave a certain way because they are labeled "10 Honors" or "College-Level 2." They are individuals with unique personality characteristics that we as teachers need to respect and nurture. Olivia blossomed on the computer screen. When she could "talk" one on one with me and share her ideas with a select few, she felt comfortable, and as that comfort level increased, her work began to show an increasing sensitivity and depth. The truth is, I got to know Olivia over that computer screen, and I feel a deep regret that, in the preceding six months in the classroom, I hadn't gotten to know her well, nor had I done what I could have to fully nurture her talents. Now I think about what I might have done differently in class to encourage the growth that instead happened in three lonely months. Certainly I could have pushed Olivia to talk more, but I know that, just as with flowers in a garden, you can't force growth. In the physical classroom, Olivia wasn't ready to bloom. Yet what for so many students was a challenging and unorthodox learning environment proved for Olivia to be the perfect place to grow at her own pace, both as a thinker and as a voice in the world. In this period of online learning, she developed the courage to send a fictional piece to the school literary magazine, where it was published and praised, and she submitted a scholarly essay on Transcendentalism to a national competition and won third prize.

I don't have an absolute answer to the question of what I could have done differently with Olivia in a traditional classroom, but I think I've learned some things from my experience with her. The most important is that whole-class discussion is not the only—nor necessarily the most important—"conversation" that goes on in my classroom. For all students, but for the quiet ones in particular, there are other, more limited human interactions that can promote both conversational skills and confidence.

In the classroom, we tend to call conversation *discussion*, and we hope that it will involve as many students as possible. That is a commendable goal, but for those students who are quiet by nature, who lack confidence in group situations, or who simply have had little experience articulating their ideas, whole-class discussion can be intimidating. Such students benefit from opportunities offered on a smaller scale that allow them to want to share their thoughts and, in the process, to develop conversational skills.

In the steady flow of emails that Olivia and I shared through the months of quarantine, I came to realize that this correspondence was for her a sort of conversation, the kind she never really had in the classroom. Her words on the screen were heartfelt and insightful, and she expressed herself with a vulnerability that her reserved demeanor didn't display. But while the ability to express oneself well via the written word is vitally important, so too is it important for young people to develop their verbal skills. Not only do I regret that Olivia never felt quite comfortable enough to routinely speak her mind in my classroom, but I also regret that her classmates never had the opportunity to hear her great ideas. We all lost something because of her silence—and likely this was the case with other studiously quiet students. The question is how to rectify this situation.

Through my computer conversations with Olivia, I came to realize that meaningful conversation with the teacher can be a first step to a wider exchange, and that verbal dialogue can begin in a written form. From my experience with Olivia, I became aware of the power my comments can have on very quiet students, and that those comments become a sort of validation that paves the way to broader communication. Though I may not be able to turn taciturn students who shy away from class discussion into animated classroom talkers, if I can increase *our* communication, that might build their confidence to a point where they begin to feel comfortable sharing an idea aloud with their peers. In the best situation, that teacher-student communication would be face to face, the two of us talking back and forth, and in the classroom, conferencing one on one about a student's writing is definitely a good place to start. But for those students who are reticent and reserved, even that exchange can be uncomfortable. We all know the students who simply nod and agree with whatever we say in hopes that we'll just go away. So, for these students, I know that the comments I write on their papers, journals, and reflections need to be especially personal and positive if I hope to give them the courage to share their ideas with a group. I've found it is also helpful to highlight on students' papers specific ideas I wish they would share with their classmates. I always encourage students to talk with me about the comments I've written on their papers, either outside of class or during in-class conferencing time, and I welcome written replies if a student prefers to write back rather than talk, trusting that eventually that written communication will naturally turn into verbal conversation. What I now believe is that, if I'm careful to offer extensive and detailed penned reactions and responses to their written work, such encouragement may be enough to help those very quiet students to "bloom." And even if that doesn't happen, more written comments between us will ensure that these students don't simply disappear from my view, overshadowed by those whose louder voices fill the classroom.

Quiet students can also benefit from opportunities that promote conversation in small groups. A natural place for such conversation is in response groups. I am deeply committed to the process writing model, and so my students meet often in established groups of four or five to share their writing and to receive feedback, in the form of questions and comments, from one another. I am adamant that this all happen through an organic conversation, and that it not be structured with worksheet-type questions to answer or checklists to complete. My rationale for this is threefold: (1) students tend to see any sort of directed response as an assignment rather than as an integral part of any writer's process, (2) unstructured response is far more authentic and addresses the unique concerns of a particular paper, and (3) students benefit from the opportunity to practice their conversational skills in these small groups.

For most of my students, response groups are one of their favorite aspects of the class. I am well aware that not every moment of response group time is spent in response, and, as I circle the room "eavesdropping," I certainly hear snippets of conversation about topics unrelated to the paper. But were an interloper to listen in on any adult writing group, I suspect they too would hear chatter about sports and shopping and the price of gas. We become better and more honest responders when we feel a human connection with those in the group, and that connection is often best achieved through natural conversation about aspects of life we have in common and things that are on our minds. In a classroom, this kind of spontaneous sharing has the added benefit of helping shy students feel more relaxed and comfortable with their peers.

Ultimately, though, response group work has to turn to actual response, and if that doesn't happen naturally, I need to insist that it begin. My students know that helpful response includes positive comments, as well as questions and concerns about parts of the work that seem confusing or incomplete. Early on in the year, response group comments are predictable—and relatively useless. I hear "It was good" echoing around the room, but nothing follows those three words. What exactly was good—and why—is a mystery to all, and no one seems to have the gumption to tackle all that was not "good."

There are various ways to approach this problem, ones that go beyond waiting it out and hoping for group dynamics to kick in. Modeling the response group process is an excellent approach, and, if a class of students is unfamiliar with the use of response groups, that is an absolutely necessary first step. When I first model a response group, I involve either the entire class or a subset of the class as responders, and I, using a piece of student writing not from the class, act as the writer. Students know that the writer's first responsibility is to inform the group of where the piece is at in terms of the draft stage and to focus responders' attention on the parts of the piece the writer has concerns about. Since I didn't actually write the piece I'm reading, I have to playact a bit, but I do give some direction, saying, for example, "I'm not sure that the opening is strong enough to attract a reader's attention," or "Please tell me if you can visualize the house.

I don't know if there needs to be more description." I then read the piece aloud. Inevitably there is silence as I finish speaking the final word—and I let students know that this is normal and not indicative of the quality of the piece. Responders need time to process their thoughts, and frequently people are unsure how to begin the conversation. That's unfortunately where the "serves all purposes" phrase "It was good" too often comes in. But the task for me now, straddling the roles of both teacher and pretend writer, is to get the responders to say something significant. If they want to praise the work, then they need to talk about a specific aspect of the work. "It's good" isn't helpful, but perhaps the final line is a clincher and ends the piece just right. Maybe the dialogue is strong and realistic and moves the whole story along. Perhaps specific words (and I'd ask them to note exactly which words) have been well chosen, or maybe there's a smooth rhythm and flow to the opening paragraph. This specific praise is far more valuable to the writer than the generic "It's good" comment, partly because it seems more sincere but, more important, it ensures that the writer won't go back to revise something that's already strong. Finally, hearing such specific positive comments builds the writer's confidence and allows them to ask for and really *hear* comments that focus on weaker parts of the piece. In this practice group, I can serve as a sort of coach to encourage students to ask questions about passages that confuse them or to offer suggestions to strengthen areas that the writer isn't satisfied with. In this modeling with a practice group, there are many stops and starts as I pause the action to talk about what we are all trying to do to help the writer improve the piece. Obviously, using an entire class of students to respond to a piece that wasn't actually written by a peer sitting there with them makes this activity somewhat artificial, but it does offer students the experience of a response group that they can modify when they work in their own small groups.

As we discuss the writing, conversation doesn't always go smoothly and students tend to offer comments that jump from one aspect of the piece to another, but I'm willing to sacrifice rigid structure for honest enthusiasm and participation. I do, however, caution students that they need to honor general rules of courtesy in conversation and avoid interrupting others or shifting attention to anything other than the writer and their work.

Students who have participated previously in response groups generally don't need this sort of modeling activity, but they do sometimes need the teacher to help them keep the conversation moving. While students meet in response groups, I continually circle about, listening to each group. Often I'll pause at a group that has either gone silent or reverted to mindless chatter, and I give the group members my full attention. Usually just my presence is enough to spark the conversation and get them back on track, but if it's not (and sometimes, when a classmate's paper shows virtually no effort, they are quiet for justifiable reasons), I'll sit down with the group to participate as though I were a group member. At the same time, I try to draw each responder into the conversation. My aim is not to micromanage the conversation by demanding that each student speak a certain number of times or that each offer a different suggestion, but rather to contribute to the process so that students can engage in productive discussion on a more personal level, one that I hope allows the quieter students to have a voice.

Another technique to help facilitate shared and serious conversation in response groups is to ask all students to end the response time by writing a brief reflection that focuses on what they heard from their responders concerning their own piece. I ask them to reflect specifically on what they heard that made them happy—in other words, what responders said made the piece successful—and to also reflect on comments and questions they intend to address as they continue to revise their work. I'm essentially asking them to recap who said what about their work, and this serves a number of purposes. It ensures that the writer truly listens to what responders say (and because students do this during class time, they can also ask for clarification from group members on things that were said), and it distills down to key points the response group conversation about the work. At the same time, it makes the responders feel a greater sense of responsibility, knowing that their comments have weight and do matter in terms of the development of the writer's work. Beyond this, these reflections allow me to see that all members of the group are contributing to the conversation. Students hold onto these reflections as they are revising their papers and use them as a way to remind themselves what they heard in response, but they then turn in the reflections with their final papers and draft work, giving me the opportunity to review the group's comments.

There are, of course, many other ways to promote small-group discussion. In what are sometimes called buzz groups, a few students work together for a specified time to discuss a question or complete a task. Often when analyzing literature, teachers use this small-group approach, which offers a low-risk way for students to share their interpretations of the work with one another. As with response groups, students can engage in both extraneous and focused conversation, which creates a relaxed environment. But I've found response groups to be most effective in creating a space where quieter students begin to truly feel comfortable participating and sharing their ideas. I think there are three basic reasons for this.

The first is that the composition of each response group remains constant. Once a group is established, the members of that group do not change. Over the course of the semester or year, students learn to trust one another and to feel at ease in each other's presence, and this growing sense of familiarity makes those less confident students feel safe. Often, in fact, students who first met in response groups form friendships that outlast the duration of the course. The more extroverted students also learn to recognize that quiet doesn't mean vacuous, and they find that when a more introverted classmate does speak, often their words are significant. This design allows each person to connect at their own pace, and so, while some students jump right into the group interaction, others take more time to feel their way into active participation.

Second, the work students do in response groups generally leads them to get to know one another on something more than a superficial level. Though I certainly use response time when students are writing analytical pieces, I find it's even more important when students write personal essays, narrative, memoir, and the like. In these creative works, the writers share pieces of themselves, and this advances and enhances the human connection that many students need to feel if they are to verbally express themselves and ultimately develop a true sense of empathy.

Finally, with response there is no right or wrong. A reader's reactions to a piece of writing are subjective, and though yes, it may take a bit of courage to express your opinion about a classmate's writing, you can't be *wrong* in what you say. For all students, but especially for those who are generally more timid or fearful of being incorrect in their ideas, the openness of response can be freeing.

Students can experience some of this through collaborative work on creative writing projects as well. I'm a big fan of list poems that small groups of students create through cooperative effort and the sharing of individual ideas. The list or catalog poem is a compilation of images and ideas presented in a list form, all typically focused on one general topic. Inspired by various writers and their works, my students write list poems about things they don't understand (see Leah Hager Cohen's *I Don't Know: In Praise of Admitting Ignorance (Except When You Shouldn't)*, about things they prefer (see Wisława Szymborska's poem "Possibilities"), and about emotions they feel (see Raymond Carver's poem "Fear"). In creating these "laundry list" poems, students find themselves contributing ideas that reveal personal feelings in a way that allows them to remain just a little bit distant—and so therefore safe. As I walk around the room listening in on groups, I hear conversations that sometimes feel like confessions, and I can almost read on the faces of those students who often hover on the edges a relief as they discover that we all struggle in one way or another. In one instance, group members talk about anxiety and the things that cause each to feel anxious and apprehensive, including physics, driving tests, and college applications. They end their list poem with these lines:

Anxiety about how I look
Anxiety about who I am
Anxiety about my anxiety

For the student who lacks confidence and too often feels they don't measure up, this sort of sharing comes as an epiphany—and a chance to bloom.

One other way quiet students sometimes find "their" voice is when they adopt the voice of someone else entirely. This has happened more than once when my students role-play. A much-loved activity for them is our version of the *Dr. Phil* show. A great deal of the literature we read involves families who suffer some sort of family dysfunction and who therefore could benefit from the attention of the good doctor. Though we've done this activity with such works as Lorraine Hansberry's *A Raisin in the Sun*, J. D. Salinger's "Teddy," and Joy Williams's "The Skater," our personal favorite is when Dr. Phil meets the Vincent family from Susan Minot's 1986 *Monkeys*, a novel based loosely on her own experiences growing up. Once we reach a point in the book when family secrets have been revealed, Dr. Phil and the Vincent parents and their seven children convene around an arrangement of desks with the doctor at the head. The rest of the class serves as the studio audience, who participate when the doctor asks for their reactions and/or questions. The students who volunteer to play the family members and Dr. Phil all quickly fall into character, and always a lively conversation follows.

One thing that fascinates me is who volunteers to be which character. Interestingly, it's often one of the quieter students who eagerly dons the hat of Dr. Phil or that of the arrogant and alcoholic Gus Vincent or his troubled wife, Rosie. I admit I frequently feel a bit of trepidation when I hand a major role to such a reserved student, but inevitably they come through. The same student who sits silently through a class discussion suddenly comes to life, firing questions with authority to the family members or defending themself against the children's accusations. Somehow, under the cloak of a new identity, certain students lose their inhibitions and join in conversation. And while this is acting and not true conversation, this sort of role-playing strategy can help to break down barriers. It's as if, once a student hears their voice applauded in the classroom, even under the guise of a fictional character, they somehow feel more able to express themself in other classroom situations. Also, as a student explained in a reflection, there's something to be said for "switching it up" in class: "Sometimes if the conversations are just really boring, I zone out which cause me not to participate. I think switching up the way we talk in class is really fun though. Like sometimes we just listen and talk about the books, but one day we did Dr. Phil which was when a lot of people participated and enjoyed freely talking."

Something I haven't yet addressed in this chapter is the issue of a "class participation" grade, particularly as motivation for participation. Frankly, such a thing is anathema to me. To begin with, I have never understood how a teacher fairly calculates such a grade. I struggle to see how we can be fully engaged in class discussion if we're busy putting check marks next to each student's name each time they speak. Does simply opening one's mouth count as participating? Does the specter of a grade encourage students to say empty and inane things, simply to achieve a quota of comments? Does the quality of one's comments have any bearing on the class participation grade? Is one insightful comment worth three "I agree with Marys"? Is saying one thing per class period enough, or should each student speak three times? And what if some students are long-winded and the bell rings before everyone has had an opportunity to participate?

All of these logistical questions make me shudder, but what really stops me is the question of what this pressure puts on the Olivias of the world. I know some would say that this is the way to motivate quiet students to speak, but that sort of pressure isn't an "incentive" I want to offer. The child who stutters, the one who struggles with ELA classes, the one who simply feels like a pariah for a million and one reasons should not have to come into my classroom, throat dry, palms sweating, and feeling the pressure to speak in order to succeed academically. Significantly, there is no option to revise in conversation. The student who struggles with a writing assignment can sit down with me for feedback and extra help and can do any number of rewrites, all of which is quite private. Talking in a class discussion comes with none of that protection, and so it's a far riskier pursuit. I *do* want my students to speak for themselves, but I don't want them to speak for a grade. The reward for good classroom conversation shouldn't be an A; it should be increased understanding—both of the topic and of those around you.

This doesn't mean, however, that I totally absolve students of personal responsibility for making their ideas known. By adolescence a person needs to accept some responsibility for establishing their place in the classroom. High school students, moreover, need to understand that the ability to speak up and make one's voice heard is essential in the adult world, whether it be in a college classroom or in the workplace. In "Silent Students Shortchange Themselves, and Others," writer Carlo Rotella offers an interesting perspective on the silent student. He explains that one of the most effective ways to learn is to "participate in conversation with flesh-and-blood human beings who form a genuine community of inquiry," and he then makes a thought-provoking observation: "Three decades in college classrooms have taught me that if you don't talk in class during the first two weeks, you're probably going to remain entirely silent for the rest of the semester. This brief period at the beginning of the semester in which students either do or don't become a person who talks in class is an unforgiving fact of academic life."

Although I think there are some differences in the high school classroom, I have to admit that Rotella's point has merit. It's true that very quickly most students establish themselves as those who speak and those who don't, and all of a teacher's best intentions may not change that latter group. Rotella's contention is that the longer a student hesitates to speak up in class, the less likely it is they ever will. He calls it "a kind of verbal writer's block." Ultimately, though he says that his method of ameliorating this situation "goes against my strong instinct to let people do what they want," he nevertheless requires students to speak every time the class meets, especially in the first weeks of class.

Though his arguments are compelling, Rotella's words have not yet persuaded me to go quite this far, but I do share this article and his findings with my students. I think even an awareness of this classroom reality can help students move past their insecurities and understand what they may be losing in their reluctance to speak in class. Moreover, this acknowledgment of the feelings many students have about speaking up in class can help alleviate some anxiety as students realize they aren't alone in their fears.

The truth too is that it can't fall entirely on the teacher to draw each student out. That's not simply a philosophical belief but a reality based on the sheer number of students in a classroom. I do, however, believe that the teacher is responsible for creating an atmosphere that encourages *all* students to participate, and that means providing a variety of activities that promote conversation within the classroom. In her reflection on the rupi kaur poem, Olivia wrote, "This poem gives me courage at the same time that it fills me with fear." Teachers need to acknowledge the fear that fills many of our students, not just the Olivias but also the Danielles and others who really do want to speak but whose hands never quite make it into the air. As teachers our job is to give these students courage by communicating the belief that *every* voice matters. Thinking back to that orchestra, not every musician gets first chair, but the music each plays is essential to the whole work. So too are the words each student speaks if we, as a class, are to make beautiful music.

4

Presentation or Conversation?

I've found that if I say what I'm really thinking and feeling, people are more likely to say what they really think and feel. The conversation becomes a real conversation.

—Carol Gilligan

"So it's like a science fair?" Jack asks. He looks quizzical, as do the twenty-seven other students in front of me.

"Pretty much," I say. "It's an opportunity for you to present *in* small groups *to* small groups and to really *talk* about what you've been researching."

A testy comment travels from the back of the room. "Why can't we just present the regular way?"

If I were being honest, my immediate response would be, "Because it's far too tedious—and time consuming—to have each of you stand in front of the room and mumble for ten minutes. Because I can't stand to see all your classmates' eyes glaze over. Because I have watched all the PowerPoints I can bear."

Those are the somewhat selfish but truthful reasons I have abandoned the "stand in the front of the room and tell us what you know" model of oral presentation. We've all experienced them. We know how painful it is to watch a student stammer and stutter because the spotlight is too much—or because they barely did a thing to prepare. We know how uncomfortable it is when another student goes on and on and there's no polite way to stop them. We've experienced how maddening it is to listen to students read, almost word for word, information that we can tell comes from a single source. And we know how exasperating it is to watch a classroom full of students sit passively, feeling no connection to the presenter or the topic, and just waiting for the bell to ring.

But these emotional reactions we have to poorly designed—and I would say poorly *assigned*—presentations have an educational basis as well. The reactions I've described reflect the problems frequently encountered when we ask students to present in front of their classmates. Often awkward and uncomfortable, students understandably lack the performance abilities that skilled presenters develop over time. When they work alone on a presentation, they don't reap the benefits that collaborative work offers, such as support, feedback, and a division of labor, and when they present in a group, one student often takes on primary responsibility, allowing others to hide in the background and shirk the work. Frequently, students don't feel fully invested in their work, so the resulting presentation is shoddy and boring, and students have no opportunity to revamp, revise, and improve the quality of the presentation. Most important, students rarely feel that anyone in the audience matters, other than the teacher.

Yet, despite all these issues, I think most of us would agree that presentations are a valuable learning activity for students, and they are certainly a staple of the ELA classroom. The skills we want students to acquire through this sort of activity will serve them well, both in the classroom and outside of it. They need to learn to ask good questions, to research various sources and determine the legitimacy of each, to sift through material and distill it down, to organize the material effectively, and to ultimately find a coherent—and appealing—way of communicating information. And all of that should happen even before they make their way to the front of the room.

The oral component of the presentation is designed to teach students to articulate their ideas well and to speak clearly, loudly, slowly, and with appropriate emphasis. It purports to train them to stand tall, to make eye contact, and to demonstrate a sense of self-confidence. It encourages them to design a visual aid and to use it effectively throughout the presentation. Ultimately, it asks them to connect with and engage a tough audience, composed of an entire class of peers, not to mention the teacher with a gradebook.

When I reread this list of all that the presentation model is supposed to achieve and all that it demands of students, frankly, I start to sweat. This is a long list of formidable goals, especially for adolescents whose self-esteem is often fragile and whose experience as presenters is limited at best. And though I noted this above, it's worth repeating: when students present in front of the class in the traditional manner, there is no chance for a redo. If the presentation flops, whether because of fear or inexperience or inadequate preparation, it's a done deal, as the teacher's grade will reflect. Though with writing assignments we recognize the need for draft work, feedback, and revision, we somehow seem to believe that a presentation exists only as a final product and that students should be able to produce work of quality in one "draft."

So what do we do—and what does this have to do with conversation in the classroom? It took many years of teaching for me to come up with an alternative approach to the typical presentation, and it's one that involves authentic human communication. I call it the "science fair" model because it replicates in many respects the way science fairs are designed, with a presenter explaining their research to small audience groups. These audience members have the opportunity to immediately ask questions and to engage in genuine conversation about the research. In my English classroom, it's not always a perfect solution, but it has definitely improved the quality of student work, and it's a model to which I am now committed. The basic foundation of this model is the idea that students present best when they are truly engaged with their audience—in other words, when they are connected in a situation that mimics the best human interaction, and that is authentic conversation.

This model begins with the selection of groups. I allow students to choose their own groups of four. My one suggestion to them is that they remember that all of us possess different talents and abilities, and while they might prefer to gravitate toward their best friends or their brightest classmates, a wiser approach would be to form a group composed of four people with various abilities. Maybe someone is a great artist, or an excellent researcher, or a good speaker, or a creative genius. Maybe someone has strong organizational skills or leadership qualities or a real thirst for knowledge. The goal, I tell my students, is to form a group that can work as an effective team because the individual group members possess different strengths. I also tell them that they will work with this same group for all the presentations they give during the semester because, as with any team, issues with group dynamics can be worked out over time—and that too is a skill students need to learn for the world beyond the classroom.

Though all four students work together to research the topic (and I give students a great deal of choice in terms of topics) and to plan the presentation, when the actual oral component begins, students present in pairs, and again, I tell them to play to one another's strengths. A weaker speaker would be wise to work with a stronger one rather than letting two extroverts pair up and leaving two introverts to muddle on alone. On the day they present, each pair has the opportunity to present three times, each time to a different small cohort of their classmates.

So then, if I had a class of twenty-eight students, there would be seven groups of four students, and within each of those seven groups, the four would have divided themselves into two presenter pairs. I typically allot two periods for presentations. On the first day, three of the seven groups present; on the second day, four do so. This plan can be adapted, based on the length of a class period and depending on the school schedule. I would suggest, however, that if there is an odd number of groups, fewer groups present on the first day when students are just learning how to set up and present in this format.

We set up stations with students' visual aids in the room (or in the hallway to allow for more space), and three groups begin to present simultaneously, with one pair from each group presenting. The remaining students who are not presenting that day or in that first round become the audience. These audience members (including those students from the pairs not presenting) split themselves into three groups, and each group goes to a different station/presentation. The presenters present, the audience (and it is a small audience of maybe six or seven students) listens, and I join one of the audience groups to listen while also timing the presentation. (I tell students earlier, when they are planning their presentations, how long they should plan to present.) When time is called, each audience group moves to the next pair of presenters and the process is repeated, and then it is repeated again, until each pair has presented three times and every audience member, myself included, has circulated through all of the presentations. We then switch presenters and the process repeats for the new pairs. If this exact plan is followed, the students not presenting that day hear the material twice. It's not always repetitive, however, because each pair presents in a slightly different way and emphasizes different aspects of the topic. Even when key material is repeated, this benefits student learning, as it's a rare student who doesn't need to hear important information more than once.

I do sometimes use a variation of this approach, especially when classes are very large. In this variation, only half the class hears the first set of presenters. At the midway point, when the pairs of presenters switch, they sit out, while the other half of the class hears the second set of presenters. Both models work, depending on the number of students in the class, the space available for part of the audience to sit out, and the students' ability to work independently while the first round of presentations is going on.

One other important note—I also ask each group to prepare a one-page handout for each audience member. The handout serves a number of purposes: (1) it helps presenters to organize and condense their key points, and so it improves the overall quality of their talk, (2) it allows audience members to focus on the conversation they can have with the presenters rather than on taking notes, and (3) it provides me with a written record of their research, thus allowing me to concentrate on their presentation skills.

As described, this design may sound confusing; in action, it is not. Students easily understand how to make a circuit through the stations, and, while I'm doing the same thing, I can keep an overall eye on the interactions between presenters and audience.

And it is that interaction that is key to this design. Yes, the presenters present, but they don't deliver a lecture or read straight from their notecards or otherwise bore their audience to death. Because the audience is there, right in front of them, in the same stance they would likely have when holding a conversation, presenters speak more naturally and seem to feel more motivated to speak well because they are *talking to* their friends. It's not unusual—or verboten—for an audience member to interrupt, to ask a question, or to seek clarification, and in fact I encourage students to engage in their learning as a true conversation. Say, for example, that Ethan and Elise know a great deal about Rachel Carson and her work *Silent Spring,* and you don't. In a "real life" conversation, you would naturally give them the floor, but you wouldn't hesitate to ask questions and to move the conversation along through your natural curiosity and your own reactions to what you've heard. This is the stuff of real conversation, and it's what I want to hear in these "presentation conversations."

So, in my Contemporary American Culture class, if a pair were presenting on the Little Rock Nine and the 1957 battle for the desegregation of Central High in Little Rock, Arkansas, I would hope, at the beginning, to hear them share basic facts with the audience about the situation and the roles President Eisenhower, Governor Orval Faubus, and the nine teenagers played in this history-changing event. But then I would hope to hear something like this:

"What finally happened to those kids? Are they still alive?"

"I heard they went on *Oprah* once."

"What's that school like now?"

"My grandmother went to school in Boston when they were busing kids to desegregate. She's told me all about it."

And even—

"Are all schools desegregated now?"

So, while the presenters are "experts" who have advanced knowledge of the topic—and it's knowledge they have acquired through the research approach we all advocate—it's not their job to simply toss that knowledge out there, but rather to engage their peers—and me—in conversation about it. The benefits of this are enormous.

First, in terms of learning, we all know that we learn best when there's a human connection. With respect to the traditional presentation model, students *know* the classmates who are presenting in front of the class, but there exists a sort of invisible barrier in that situation. Students are expected to sit quietly and "soak up" knowledge until the presentation concludes and the presenter or teacher says, "Any questions?" By then, students typically have lost track of what they were confused about or interested in earlier in the presentation. There's no give-and-take and no real opportunity to engage with the presenter. But when students are almost nose to nose with the presenter, it becomes a much more human interaction, one that allows for the exchange of ideas. Presenters begin to recognize the aspects of their talk that most interest their audience, as well as those that confuse them, and, just as in any conversation, they can clarify points and encourage more involvement. In the best-case scenario, presenters feed off the interest of the audience and grow more confident and animated.

Second, the presenters themselves do a significantly better job of presenting. They see this as a situation in which they are expected *to talk to* their peers, and so they refrain from writing the sort of stilted monologues that typically get read from notecards. They're far less likely to misappropriate material from their sources because they know their peers will recognize "borrowed" material and language that isn't their own. They realize too that they can't count on simply relying on a script. In this model, the conversation can go in many directions, so presenters need to be well versed in all areas of the topic. Because the path of the presentation isn't entirely in the speakers' control, they have to prepare more thoroughly and truly *know* their material. I will say too that it's rare for a pair of presenters to be unprepared for their presentation or to put insufficient effort into it, because no one wants to endure three rounds of failure, especially in front of their peers.

Last, but significantly, this approach allows for student growth and improvement. Predictably, the first time a pair presents, the presentation is a bit shaky. They may have planned too much or too little material to present effectively in the time frame. They aren't yet aware of what aspects of the topic may be confusing to the audience. They haven't established an easy rhythm with each other, and they may not have figured out how to best use their visual aids. These are all things that happen when students present once in front of the whole class, but, in that case, there's no possibility of redemption. But when we use this science fair model, I can allow a few minutes after the first pair's presentation to give them the chance to regroup—in effect, to revise. So the second time they present, the presentation is considerably better, and by the third time it's usually strong and polished. When the pairs switch positions, I also give them a minute or two to talk with each other so that the first pair can share the benefit of their experience with the second pair that is about to present. All of this rethinking, revising, and readjusting—all mirroring the draft work, response, and revision we put into writing assignments—is vital if want our students to really learn *how* to present. Like any other skill, speaking with an audience takes practice, and through this model, students have multiple opportunities to improve the quality of their work and to grow more comfortable with the experience of presenting, all within the framework of one research project. I see this as an efficient use of time as students attempt to achieve mastery.

This is a design that could easily be used with a variety of presentation topics. While my Contemporary American Culture students study all aspects of culture, including history, economics, literature, art, and music, and their presentations reflect this, the science fair model would work equally well in general literature classes. For example, I know there are classes where students, either individually or in pairs, are assigned to create a presentation on a writer, which they then present to the entire class. The teacher's intent is to familiarize students with a number of writers while allowing the presenter(s) to gain in-depth knowledge. While this intent is admirable, the truth is, students typically remember very little of what they hear in this steady stream of "front of the room" presentations, especially when the presentations themselves are fairly repetitious in form and type of content. But if this were done in a science fair design, with four presenters per writer, students could more easily engage with presenters and likely feel more comfortable asking questions about those writers who particularly interest them. The teacher could also decide to group the three or four presentations in a way that emphasized connections between certain writers (e.g., time periods, themes, styles, etc.), thereby creating an easier way for students to remember these writers. Moreover, when using the science fair design, students tend to become more creative, avoiding the basic poster or PowerPoint. Perhaps a student would dress as the writer and take on their persona. The group might take this further and create a talk show segment in which the writer is interviewed. Maybe a group would play a recording of the poet reading their work or design their own choral reading. Because this design takes far fewer class periods than the traditional "front of the room" model, teachers might even decide there was time for students to read, in advance of the presentations, a poem or excerpt by each of the writers that students have chosen to present, thereby making all students feel more invested in all of the presentations. Obviously, the number of writers to whom students would be introduced is reduced using the four-person presentation design rather than the individual or pair model, but this, I believe, is a clear instance of quality over quantity.

I'm always trying to find other ways to shape research-based assignments into conversation-based activities. Years ago a sociologist friend of mine came to talk to my students about the work sociologists do and the research methods they practice. Over time, I kept coming back to one particular thing he spoke about, and that was the collaboration in which sociologists often engage as they share research and data in their pursuit of valid conclusions. This then became the idea behind one of my favorite—and one of my students' favorite—projects, called Chasing the Dream: Researching the Meaning of the American Dream. This entire project, with step-by-step instructions and additional material, can be accessed through NCTE's ReadWriteThink website (Rubenstein). For purposes of this chapter, however, I want to focus on aspects of the project that promote authentic conversation and the skills that accompany it.

In my Contemporary American Culture class, we study the concept of the American Dream because it's so central to American culture. But certainly, even in more solely literature-based classes, the idea of the pursuit of the American Dream is an important theme. It's integral to *The Great Gatsby*, *The Grapes of Wrath*, *Invisible Man*, *Death of a Salesman*, and other canonical works that many of us teach. This project can be used to deepen students' understanding of the American Dream as well as to encourage their interest in it while allowing them to engage in authentic research and real conversation.

At the center of this project is an interview. Each student has to interview a person on the meaning of the American Dream and on their own pursuit of the Dream. What makes this more interesting is that each student is assigned a decade, and the student must find an individual to interview who came of age in that particular decade. We define *coming of age* as the point at which a person becomes financially independent of their parents.

To determine what decade each student's interview must address, I have students randomly draw lots from an envelope; each paper drawn from the envelope has a specific decade on it. The number of students per group or decade depends on the number of students in the class and the number of decades you want them to explore. It's also important to take into consideration the likelihood of a student finding a person of a certain decade to interview. Though I always want students to look at the American Dream as far back as the 1950s, realistically it's getting harder these days to expect students to find an interviewee who came of age seventy years ago—though when it happens, it produces amazing results. To accomplish that, you might think of having students interview residents of local nursing homes or assisted living residences. But generally now I ask students to interview people from the 1960s through the present, which provides a wide sample of interviewees, all of whom came of age and lived, and are living, their lives under different circumstances. If I include six decades, I can easily accommodate a class of thirty with five in each decade group.

Having already spent class time discussing the concept of the American Dream and how it relates to works we are reading, we then as a class brainstorm questions we might want to ask our pool of interviewees about the American Dream. I put these questions on the board for students to record and adapt as appropriate, emphasizing that they shouldn't simply run through these questions with their interviewee, but rather use them as a framework for the information they want to collect. These questions might include such things as:

- When did you come of age? What marked that moment for you?
- What is your ethnic background? Religion? Social class? Education?

- At the time you came of age, how did you define the American Dream?
- Do you think your definition or understanding of the American Dream was similar to that of your peers? Can you elaborate?
- Is your definition or understanding of the American Dream the same now as it was when you came of age? If it has changed, please explain in what ways.
- Has your definition of the American Dream changed at various times throughout the course of your lifetime? If so, how?
- Do you feel you've achieved the American Dream? Why do you feel that way?
- Do you believe the American Dream has meaning today in 20__? Why or why not?

Once we have established a list of potential questions, we begin talking about interviewing techniques. This is a significant part of this portion of the overall project. It's critical to remember that students these days generally are not comfortable talking one on one with another human being, particularly one who isn't a peer. As one of my students wrote in a freewrite about conversation, "Many people don't want to talk to others because we've grown up not actually having to talk to a lot of people." This idea is echoed by many other students in their own freewrites. A senior wrote, "Nowadays kids have no face to face social skills. People can't look people in the eye anymore."

If this is the case, then it's imperative that we help students learn how to talk to one another, in this case in the context of an interview. My students and I talk about simple human courtesy, which I've found is not so simple for adolescents these days, many of whom have never learned rules of basic etiquette. We discuss that there is a difference between interviewing a friend or family member versus a boss or another adult acquaintance in terms of formality, but that in any case, human civility prevails. Some of the things I address are fundamentals of human interaction, but these things aren't always obvious to teenagers today. Among the points I address:

- Don't interrupt.
- Don't dominate the conversation.
- Don't check your phone or otherwise indicate disinterest in the conversation.
- Use appropriate language.

- Think before you speak.
- Use basic courtesy, words like *thank you*, *please*, and *excuse me*.
- Be nice.

And yes, look the person in the eye.

Beyond these "rules" of human communication, however, is something more elusive, and that is the *art* of conversation. This, I tell my students, means truly focusing on the person with whom you are having a conversation. To practice this skill, we often role-play conversations, with one student acting as interviewer and the other the interviewee. I ask students to choose a topic of mutual interest to them, such as soccer, science fiction, or video games, and the class, modeling the American Dream project, helps to compile a list of relevant questions. When we role-play the interview, predictably there are students acting as the interviewers who simply run through the list of questions they've decided on. For each question, they jot down an answer, either literally in a notebook or apparently figuratively in their heads, and then move on to the next question, never seeking further development and never exhibiting anything close to genuine human interest or curiosity. As a result, this exchange between interviewer and interviewee never becomes a true conversation, and it never produces interesting material—and it's usually over in a matter of minutes. This is the aspect of the interview that students really struggle with, and they seem unable to figure out how to create a genuine conversation.

So I tell students to slow down the conversation, ask specific questions that go on to develop a general answer in further depth (e.g., "So you're a soccer goalie and you love it. How did you get started as a goalie?"), and truly *listen* to the responses. This capacity to generate meaningful, in-depth conversation is a skill that students need to learn if they are to become successful communicators. In certain respects, it's a skill that's not so different from that of developing the topic sentence of a paragraph with sufficient supporting detail. But what I really want is for something far more natural to happen, something that is far more "real" than this structured planning of questions and subquestions. What I want my students to ultimately develop through role-playing—and eventually their own interviewing—is both the ability and the *desire* to listen to another human being, to enter into that person's life, and to become engrossed in their ideas and perceptions. Quite simply, I want them to care about someone else's world.

I think we would all admit that we are not a society of listeners. We speak over one another, we bluster and bluff, and we feel the need to make ourselves heard. This is true for both verbal communication and the communication that happens through social media. Sometimes I'll ask students, "Who listens to you, really *listens* to you?," and they struggle to answer. Maybe there is one trusted friend, and sometimes, happily, a parent or beloved grandparent. But the list is never long, and students seem genuinely surprised by that. They also admit that they particularly treasure the relationships they have with those who *do* listen. Listening, like speaking, is a skill and an art, and it's one that develops through steady practice and patience. Students understand when I tell them that in order to truly listen, you have to be present and in the moment. You have to give the person to whom you are talking your undivided attention. You have to screen out distractions and give the conversation your entire focus. This isn't easy for young people, or for people of any age, in a society where multitasking is a common and lauded practice. You also need to listen with both an open heart and an open mind, shutting down that tendency we have to react and judge in knee-jerk fashion. When you listen well, you are focusing on the speaker's words, not aggressively planning the point you want to respond with. You're not sparring; you're sharing, and often learning happens as a result. And, I remind students, when you listen attentively, you also notice tone of voice, body language, and facial expressions, and you process these auditory and visual clues as you shape the conversation. When I talk about these things, I keep asking students to reflect on that person who listens to them best and to recollect conversations they have had with this person in order to see how valid these ideas are.

When we are engaged in real conversation, when we don the hat of listener or are fortunate enough to have someone really listen to us, we don't even think about these things. They happen naturally, and they all contribute to the quality of the conversation. For adolescents, it's difficult to suddenly have to be cognizant of all these facets and features of conversation and to integrate them into the exchange—and, as I'm always telling my students, it *is* an exchange, a give-and-take of words and ideas. But if we can even introduce an *awareness* of these actions that promote good conversation, then we have taught our students something important, and we can work to reinforce this learning though consistent opportunities for classroom conversation.

Once students have practiced interviewing techniques and feel comfortable tackling their own interviews, I send them out to talk with their chosen subject. Not surprisingly, many choose to interview a family member who came of age in an earlier decade, but what *is* often surprising, especially to the students themselves, is what they learn about a parent, uncle, aunt, or grandparent. When the interview is done well, when the student gives their interviewee their full attention and asks about those things that make them truly curious, sometimes surprises—and even secrets—emerge. Though certainly adolescents know some family history, the stories families share are often repeated, becoming a body of family lore, and children tend to not be curious about much beyond those familiar stories. But through these interviews, teenagers come to see their parents and other relatives as young people with dreams, and they see how these dreams did—or did not—play out. They come to recognize the struggles we all face in the pursuit of our dreams, as well as the compromises we must sometimes make. When, at a later point, I ask students to write a reflection on these interviews, many comment on how much they learned about their families, and it's not unusual for some to describe a newfound closeness or connection. This is the power of conversation.

Even when students choose to interview people who aren't as close to them, perhaps a coach, a boss, a teacher, or a family friend, they always come away from the interview with a deeper understanding of another individual, and often a sense of connection. There's a realization that, despite our difference in backgrounds, ethnicity, religion, or class, we have many shared feelings and experiences. This, I think, is both eye-opening and comforting to adolescents who are on the verge of coming of age themselves and facing all the challenges that entails.

So the first part of this Chasing the Dream activity promotes conversational skills as well as authentic and interesting research. But there is a second component of the project that is equally important in terms of both encouraging conversation and challenging students to hone other research skills. Once students have completed their interviews, they write a two- to three-page draft of that interview. This isn't a transcript but rather a narrative that captures the interviewee's response in story. One important note: Because students will be sharing personal information with others in the class, I instruct them to be certain, before they begin the interview, that their interviewee is aware of how this material will be used and has agreed to share this information. I also suggest that students change the interviewee's name or use initials to further protect their subjects' privacy.

Armed with their written narratives, students meet with the other students in the class whose interviewees came of age in the same decade. All students who interviewed a person who came of age in the 1960s form one circle, the 1970s another circle, and so on. Within these small groups, students share their stories. They sometimes find, as other group members ask for elaboration and clarification, that they have omitted important details, so they are able to identify revisions they need to make—and sometimes follow-up interviews they need to conduct—before the interview is in final draft form and ready to be handed in. When all the interviews have been presented, students then discuss the data and begin to draw conclusions about the meaning of the American Dream for people of that particular decade. Though obviously it's a small sample (and we discuss that clear limitation), this is true research with findings gleaned from their own interviews. The process of drawing conclusions promotes both friendly and academic conversation. I tell them that it isn't necessary for all students to come to the same conclusion, and that interpretation of data may differ. However, students must use the actual material they have shared to support whatever conclusions they draw.

The conversation students have is usually lively and thoughtful, and they seem fascinated both by the individual stories and by the connections among them. As they talk, I wander from group to group, listening and cautioning students to not settle for easy conclusions but to examine the data closely. I'm likely to hear an exchange such as the following.

"So my interviewee came of age when he went to Vietnam in 1968," a student says. "He said his dream was just to come back alive. He didn't really think about what he wanted after that."

"I guess it was different for women," the girl next to him says. "The person I interviewed was eighteen when she got married in 1963." There's something close to a gasp from the group. "She said she wanted to go to college, but her father would only pay for her brothers."

"That's kind of like my great-aunt," a boy chimes in. "She wanted to be a psychiatrist, but she said women didn't do that then, so she ended up being a teacher. She said she always regrets that she didn't go after her dream."

"Wouldn't it be weird if it were like that now?" the fourth member of the group pipes in. "I mean, if girls just had to be teachers or nurses or secretaries?"

And suddenly the conversation (and it is *real* conversation) among the five group members goes off into a discussion of the roles of women and the expectations society places on both sexes. This is what I want to happen. I want my students to engage in conversation with their peers that allows them to express views, share ideas, and use facts and experience to illuminate all of this. On one level, I want them to do what scholars do when they share their research, but on another, I want them to do what human beings do when they want to connect, and that is talk to each other.

One last portion of this project gives students another opportunity to converse, this time in a large group. When each student's final paper is completed (and that paper includes the revised draft of the interview narrative, two pages of conclusions drawn from the data, and a one-page statement of the individual student's own perception of the American Dream), the students meet as a whole class to compare their findings among all the decades and to determine whether—and how—the pursuit of the American Dream has changed over time. We sit as a class and each decade group presents its overall conclusions, with each member of the group given a chance to speak and to offer their own interpretation. Generally, I don't have to say much, a hallmark of a good classroom conversation. The conversation ball flies from one student to another, and, while each group is eager to talk about "their" interviewees, they are equally interested in listening to the findings of other groups and intrigued by the differences they hear among young people who came of age in very different times. Though certain students are sometimes hesitant to speak when we have whole-class discussion, that reluctance seems to disappear in this group conversation, partly because students feel confident about the material since it's truly their own work and they feel comfortable explaining and defending it, and partly because they have had the opportunity to talk about it first in a small group.

Though this is only one project, it affords students three different opportunities to engage in serious and stimulating conversation, each time in a different format. There is first the one-on-one interview, then the small-group exchange, and finally the whole-group discussion. In effect, this provides a series of building blocks as students acquire comfort and skill in their ability to engage in meaningful conversation. Today's students find the one-on-one interview the most daunting, so that part of the project requires the most preparation. But part of the beauty of this project is that by the end, students' comfort level with conversation has increased almost organically.

Though I have not yet implemented this design for a topic other than that of the American Dream, I can easily imagine how it could be used. In connection with literature that focuses on coming of age, students could seek out people who came of age in different decades to see how that moment has shifted throughout the decades, especially now when we've come to accept the idea of an extended adolescence. Students reading dystopian literature might interview people about the societal challenges and changes they've encountered and then compare their responses and concerns. But whatever the chosen topic of the activity, it's the *design* that works to get students fully involved in their learning. It allows them to develop conversational skills, and this airing—and sharing—of ideas extends our curiosity about the world, allowing us to enter into worlds that are different from our own and ultimately growing into more tolerant and compassionate people.

In terms of interviewing, one exceptional resource available to teachers and students is StoryCorps. Launched in New York City in 2003 with a "storybooth" in Grand Central Terminal, this nonprofit organization has as its goal "to preserve and share humanity's stories in order to build connections between people and create a more just and compassionate world" ("About Story Corps"). To achieve this goal, "StoryCorps has given a quarter of a million Americans the chance to record interviews about their lives, to pass wisdom from one generation to the next, and to leave a legacy for the future. It is the largest single collection of human voices ever gathered. These powerful stories illustrate our shared humanity and show how much more we share in common than divides us" ("Discover StoryCorps"). The website offers extraordinary examples of people telling their stories through authentic conversations. These interviews, involving Americans from all across the country, are archived at the Library of Congress and present a vivid portrait of the diversity of American life and the struggles and celebrations inherent in that life. Recordings include LGBTQ+ stories, family histories, a military initiative for service members and their families, and a wide range of diverse voices. One particularly interesting program named One Small Step was started in 2018, providing a place for people with opposing political views to interact and record an interview with each other, in order "to break down boundaries created by politics and remember our shared humanity. To remind us that we have more in common than divides us and that treating those with whom we disagree with decency and respect is essential to a functioning democracy" ("Discover StoryCorps").

Simply listening to these varied stories has an impact on students. As they hear the speakers interact, students experience American life through the eyes of others, and they come to realize that ordinary people like themselves have compelling stories to tell—if only we would take the time to listen. These recordings remind students of the power of conversation and of the empathy and understanding that come with it. I encourage my student to listen to some of the recordings as they work on their Chasing the Dream interviews, but I also use these stories in other classroom situations, especially to connect "real life" stories with those described in fictional pieces we read.

Students can take this further and even become personally involved in the StoryCorps project by participating in an interview with a person of their choice. Interviews can be conducted at a StoryCorps recording site or through StoryCorps Connect, a videoconferencing approach developed because of the COVID-19 pandemic. Detailed information on these opportunities and all of the StoryCorps activities and stories is available on the StoryCorps website, along with specific tips and techniques to get a conversation moving.

There are certainly many more ways for students to demonstrate their learning through the power of conversation. What I think is most important, however, is to always keep in mind that a demonstration of learning needs to go beyond an audience of one—the teacher—and to help students recognize the value of sharing knowledge. Knowledge always provokes more questions, and that's what happens when students can talk with their classmates about what they have learned. Curiosity is at the core of true learning, and conversation stimulates curiosity and the exchange of ideas, or as Edith Wharton would say, "the only air worth breathing" (163).

5

"Don't Put Words in My Mouth"

As far as playing jazz, no other art form, other than conversation, can give the satisfaction of spontaneous interaction.

—*Stan Getz*

A curious thing began happening in my classroom not long ago. Discussion that once bounced and tumbled among students, often lacking much semblance of connection between ideas, suddenly began to be punctuated by a few repetitious phrases: "Piggybacking on what ________ said . . . ," "Adding on to what ________ said . . . ," "In connection with that last point. . . ." At first I was heartened by this somewhat sophisticated exchange with its use of smooth transitions, and I suspect that more than once I nodded encouragingly to the speaker. But the more I listened, really *listened,* I began to realize that these phrases were oddly empty, and in fact often pointless. Angie wasn't building on what Lucas said about Ethan Frome's tragic flaw; she was explaining why she felt sorry for Mattie Silver. Alex had nothing to add about the humor in his classmate's essay; he wanted to talk about the opening of his own. Emily appeared not to have heard a word of what Alyssa said because her "connection" was a total disconnect.

I call this new trend "template talk," and it frustrates me in much the same way the printed templates students follow to write their essays do. Certainly I applaud organization, and I work to guide discussion that moves logically and allows students to follow one another's trains of thought and build on them. But the mere interjection of a handy transitional phrase doesn't on its own do that, any more than a clear topic sentence ensures that the material in the subsequent paragraph will support it.

So I began to ask my students about this practice. How many of them used these phrases in class discussion? Where and when had they learned them? What did they see as the purpose of such phrases?

Not surprisingly, many looked taken aback by my questions, likely uncertain as to why I would question something so . . . constructive, maybe sophisticated, or at least innocuous. They stumbled over their responses and had to think hard to determine why it was they spoke as they did. It turned out that most of my students learned this practice back in middle school. Because I teach in a regional school, my students come from five different towns, so their middle school education often varies quite a bit. It appeared that some teachers in some middle schools were teaching students to use these phrases in discussion, and I'm sure their attempts were well intended. But most of my students who had been trained in the use of such introductory words somehow failed to grasp the real purpose of these phrases. They didn't seem to understand that speakers introduce such phrases when they intend to build on a comment with additional information or want to question or take exception to that specific idea. I think of Abby, one of my favorite sophomores, who grinned with an absolute lack of guile when I asked, "So why do you use these phrases?" and replied, "Because it makes me sound smart."

And it does. It initially makes a student sound smart and connected and into the discussion—and then it becomes meaningless filler. My students laughed, albeit shamefacedly, at the honesty of Abby's words, and they echoed her response. Many had been taught to preface their words in class discussion with these transitions, and they did as they were told. Now in my class they are struggling to learn when and how to use such expressions, and they have become quite deft at challenging one another when the words are hollow.

"Hey, you didn't add anything to what Jack was talking about!" someone will call out, and the "Adding to what Jack said" speaker has to do one of two things. They can refocus their thoughts and respond to Jack's comments, or they can hand the conversation back to those who are in fact reacting to Jack's comments and wait for a reasonable place to turn the talk to the topic they wish to pursue. Doing either of those things, I assure my students, doesn't just make you *sound* smart; it makes you smart.

Too frequently in classrooms, discussion is scripted by specific structured practices. But sometimes the carefully controlled techniques we use to promote discussion in our classrooms can instead limit that discussion. Take, for example, Think-Pair-Share, a technique we have all likely used, maybe more often than we should if our students' groans when they hear these three words are any indication. The idea behind this strategy is an excellent one: it asks students to think before they speak, thereby giving every student time to process thoughts and formulate ideas. By pairing students, all get a chance to speak, even the quiet ones who hesitate or refuse to raise their hands in whole-group discussion.

And as they talk in these pairs, there is supposedly an active exchange of intelligent ideas—except it doesn't always work that way.

We're reading *The Catcher in the Rye*. "What is it with those ducks?" I ask. "Why does Holden worry about where the ducks go in the winter?" I direct my students to "think, pair, share." I watch them, wishing I could see a thought bubble over each of their heads, wondering if in any of those bubbles a duck might appear. After allowing a minute or two dedicated to thinking, I encourage students to share with a partner, and they turn, often half-heartedly, to the closest person they can find, whereupon an uneasy silence generally ensues until someone in the pair says something. Then, sometimes, conversation on the topic occurs—and when it does, I'm thrilled. But more often, the second partner mumbles, "Yeah," and the two grow quiet, or the conversation I hear isn't about ducks and disillusionment but about last night's hockey game or a new YouTube video. The problem is, I've structured the conversation for them. However well intended the Think-Pair-Share technique may be, the reality is that most students see it as this: You listen to the prompt, you quickly think of something to say, you say it to the person next to you, and you're done. Even in adult workshops, I've seen this happen, and I've been guilty of participating in such disasters. The Think-Pair-Shares I've been a part of in conference sessions generally quickly veer off the topic the presenter has given us to something more appealing to the two of us, something maybe a little like sports scores and restaurant reviews. And that might be okay *if* those sorts of first exchanges relax the barriers between the pair and get them talking. Maybe once comfortable and connected with each other, the two will naturally segue into the topic at hand and have a genuine conversation about it. But in the two to five minutes usually allotted for the "share" part of this activity, there's no time for that to happen. The timed structure of the strategy ultimately defeats the potential for organic conversation.

Even the final step of the Think-Pair-Share activity, when pairs share their ideas with the whole group, often fails to produce the anticipated results. Let's say a pair does talk about those ducks and comes up with an interesting idea, perhaps that the ducks represent Holden's loneliness and sense of isolation. It doesn't take much for another pair (or two or three pairs) to decide that their response doesn't measure up to that thoughtful interpretation, and so it becomes all too easy to simply say, "Yeah, we agree with what Charlie and Carolyn said." To ask that agreeable pair to then elaborate on their response is somewhat unrealistic, because, in a couple of minutes, how much development of the topic could there have been? A quick Think-Pair-Share simply doesn't give students time to talk, to *really* talk and share their ideas, ideas that may go beyond the scope of the teacher's prompt but that may matter to them.

Teachers can use any number of discussion starters, all of which are meant to promote good discussion, and there are times when they can be used effectively (see Chapter 8, "Tricks of the Trade"). But to rely on them, to convince ourselves that we are encouraging authentic conversation in the classroom through their use, is specious, and often a deterrent to any authentic communication among students. As Celeste Headlee writes in *We Need to Talk*, "I can't give you specific words to use or phrases to repeat that will make your conversations better. There's no such thing as a conversational skeleton key" (87). Yet some teachers insist that students use transitional phrases like those described earlier or offer their students an array of "conversational stems," phrases such as "I heard you say ________," "Did you mean ________?," and "Can you rephrase ________?" and require their students to use these phrases in class discussion.

Again, there's nothing wrong with teaching students the importance of asking good questions or seeking clarification in a discussion. Certainly, too, on a basic level, students need to learn the etiquette of conversation and may need to be reminded how to politely ask a speaker to repeat or clarify an idea. But the rigid and required use of these stems and starters, often presented in handouts with charts and patterns that group and categorize their purpose (add on stems, reasoning stems, disagreement stems, etc.) in order to facilitate conversation, makes the effort feel as though students are leaning a foreign language. And perhaps they are. Perhaps they are actually learning for the first time the language of conversation, but it, like any foreign language, is best learned by doing, *not* by mimicking how to do it. I'm sure many of us studied French or Spanish for years in high school and college and were likely good students, garnering As and maybe even able (perhaps with the assistance of a dictionary) to read pages of *L'Etranger* or *Don Quixote*. Then one day we found ourselves in Paris or Madrid, and suddenly we realized we were totally unable to communicate with any native speaker. But if we were lucky enough to stay in the country long enough to fumble our way through many actual conversations, we likely learned more in that span of time than we did in all our years of classroom study. In some respects, the persistent use of conversation stems and discussion starter phrases is very much like the use of memorized dialogues often employed in language classes. Though I can still repeat many of these dialogues, my ability to actually converse in French is limited because my study of the language was so structured and I had little chance to put words together on my own.

Were students simply introduced to these stems and starters as *possible* ways to ease their entry into a conversation, I would have less of a problem with them. But in some classrooms, these conversation stems and frames are pasted to students' desks in order for students to routinely use them in class discussion. In some situations, students are even directed to check off each individual conversation starter as they use it, as a way to "practice" employing all of them. For some students, then, the process of looking at the list and determining how to create a sentence using the stem becomes the primary task, and the content of the conversation, what the student really wants to add to the conversation, is secondary. I have seen teaching videos in which students say emphatically, "I look at the list *every* time I talk," and I wonder what happens when that student moves beyond their desk and tries to engage in conversation.

Another discussion strategy, used most often in elementary grades but one that sometimes extends to secondary school classrooms, involves the use of hand signals—thumbs up, stacked fists, finger-pointing, and the like. These visual signals are designed to encourage participation and collaboration in conversation. By following these hand signals, teachers and students know such things as who is agreeing or disagreeing with the speaker or who has a thought to add to the conversation. Perhaps for young children or those struggling with language, this approach has merit, but for older students it becomes an artificial device divorced from the activity of genuine conversation.

Much has been made of "Accountable Talk" in recent years. As described by Lauren B. Resnick and colleagues in "Accountable Talk," students hold themselves responsible for getting the facts right, for thinking through challenges together, and for following rules that encourage participation (such as respectful listening) (17). The authors explain, "Rather than passively absorbing the small body of knowledge the teacher is able to transmit, students can learn reasoning skills by talking and arguing their way through problems to conclusions and solutions" (14). These are worthy aims and are much the same as what I see as the goals of good conversation, wherein participants share ideas and grow in understanding. But the authors then go on to describe specific classroom practices involved in Accountable Talk, which include assigning discussion roles to individual students (e.g., evaluator or summarizer), as well as advocating the use of sentence openers. This is where I back away, and there is a fundamental reason for this. "The goal of Accountable Talk is to develop students' ability to think. By practicing the skills and habits of argumentation through social interaction, students learn to reason" (17). This goal, while commendable, is not what I am pursuing in my advocacy of classroom talk. My primary reason for encouraging consistent opportunities for conversation in the classroom is for students to learn to connect and communicate face to face. Yes, I believe conversation will improve their ability to think, to reason, and to achieve academic success, but my priority is to restore to our students an essential human ability that is at the heart of our humanity—the ability to look each other in the eye and speak what is in our minds and hearts in words that are our own.

I know that when we as teachers train our students in specific discussion techniques we have only good intentions. We want to get the proverbial conversational ball rolling, we want to promote productive discussion, and, in particular, we want to help those students who, for a variety of reasons, struggle to join in the larger classroom conversations. We mean well when we, in effect, put words in our students' mouths, and there are occasions that and students who may require some such direction. But sometimes I think we have another reason for doing this. We are afraid of silence.

Silence, however, is an important component of conversation. As Cicero wrote, "Silence is one of the great arts of conversation." Who among us hasn't sat in a department meeting wishing a colleague would just be quiet for a minute, or wanting to suggest that the group take a breath to think before the conversation continues? Students are no different from adults. They need the benefit of silence in order to proceed with good discussion. This is different from that "wait time" we've all been trained to utilize. "Wait time," as defined by Mary Budd Rowe in 1972, encouraged a minimum three-second hiatus between a teacher's question and the first student response in order to improve the quality of student response (J. McCarthy). The later work of Robert Stahl suggested an extension of this time as a period of "think time," which is "a distinct period of uninterrupted silence by the teacher and all students so that they both can complete appropriate information processing tasks, feelings, oral responses, and actions" (2). Yet as long as measured silent seconds can seem to the teacher who stands in that silence at the front of the class, it often isn't enough time for students to fully process ideas and to put their own thoughts into coherent words. Though a teacher may use this technique skillfully in the classroom to promote more answers and "better" answers, neither wait time nor think time serves the same function as silence. Encouraging silence isn't about us giving students the time to figure out the answer. Silence is about three things:

1. Creating space for students to take in, respect, and process the words they have heard, whether from the teacher or their classmates
2. Allowing students the opportunity to pull together their own thoughts without the chaos of conversation in their ears
3. Acknowledging—and applauding—the reality that students may say, "I don't know"—and nothing more

A classroom is a busy place, full of energy and activity and numerous distractions. Whether the teacher is directing instruction or students themselves are generating questions and comments, there is a lot to take in. There are times in my classroom when I feel like a ringmaster of a three-ring circus, and I know that both my students and I are struggling to fully experience the words flying from one corner of the room to the other. Even when a discussion is more measured and "civilized," I'm very aware that students are likely hearing thoughts and ideas they have never before considered and that they need time and space to contemplate these new concepts and possibilities. All veteran teachers know the feeling of trying, in one's head, to stay one step ahead of what is being said in class discussion in order to help shape and smooth the conversational thread. I think we'd all agree that's not an easy task, even when we know the material inside out and, after years of experience, have a sense of where students may take the material. But students come to a lesson or discussion like a circus audience, new to the performance and trying to take in all the action at once, and that can be overwhelming. If only we could freeze that action, suspend the trapeze artists in mid-air, put the brakes on the clown car, and halt the lion's roar.

The best I can do to achieve this in my classroom is to imagine that I possess a pause button. When class discussion spirals and I'm hearing a chaotic conglomeration of thoughts and questions, when it seems that every student is speaking in a vacuum with little awareness of what anyone else is saying, and when too many faces are looking panicked or perplexed, that's when I hit that button.

"Stop," I say. "Everyone pause. And now breathe. Just take a deep breath and breathe." And then we sit in silence. I don't time it. I don't chart it. I respect it. And my students have learned to respect these periods of silence too. In these moments of silence, I can feel the air in the room decompress. I can start to see, in my students' body language, a sense of relaxation, and in their eyes a look of calm focus appears. Once that happens, I tell them to just sit and think quietly about what they were hearing or thinking or wondering when we paused the action. In that silence, students have space to think more deeply about the ideas they've heard ricocheting around them, and they can begin to frame their own thoughts in response. I allot no set time for this silence. There is a lovely line in Lorraine Hansberry's play *A Raisin in the Sun* where the character Asagai says, "Never be afraid to sit awhile and think" (137). Awhile. Simply awhile. And so we take whatever time we need.

This strategy is one I typically explain to my students early in the school year. I want them to understand that, in this case, the word *Stop* is not a reprimand. It's not me saying, "Be quiet. Sit down. Pay attention," or any such command a teacher might use with an unruly group. These pauses are, rather, a gift—a gift of respite—and I want students to appreciate this time of silence, a time when it's good and right to say nothing because, as Cicero tells us, silence is part of the art of conversation.

Sometimes, when we're ready to break the silence, we can restart the action where we left off and resume with a relaxed focus that allows meaningful conversation to proceed. In such cases, when students have used the period of silence to reconsider ideas, reframe arguments, and often resettle emotions, productive conversation can begin. Other times, however, the pre-pause chaos was so great, with the conversation veering in so many directions, that we all need to regroup to know where to even start again.

One way to do this is to ask students to "recapture" the ideas that were being discussed when we paused the action. As students call out each separate idea, I put a word or brief phrase on the board to allow us all to visually see the thoughts we were having. Perhaps a discussion of William Faulkner's "A Rose for Emily" had originally started with a student's question about the meaning of the title, but from there the conversation veered in many directions. *Isn't red about love? Or is it anger? I know roses mean love. Did Emily love Homer? Did he love her? How long would it take for Homer to rot anyway? Why didn't they get married? Is there really a rose? What's with Tobe? Did he kill Homer? Why'd he leave?* I take these kernels of thought—words or phrases like *Tobe? Symbolism of the color red? Meaning of flowers? Decomposition?*—from all those questions and put them on the board to help us remember what we wanted to talk about and also to help us visualize how there might be connections between ideas that, on the surface, seem disconnected. This process doesn't impose an artificial structure on the conversation, but rather it permits students to see possibilities of how one idea might naturally lead to the next. And if we don't get to all the ideas that students want to discuss in that class period, it's easy enough for me to jot down the remaining ideas or snap a picture of the board to guarantee that when the next class begins, we can pick up where we left off.

Throughout this process, I remind my students of the benefit of silence, and I ask them to keep going back to the thoughts that were in their heads when we sat quietly. Oddly, those moments are memorable to them, perhaps because silence is a rare commodity in our society these days. In a world where we are all buffeted by newscasts, entertainment options, and the ongoing chatter of social media 24/7, where everyone seems to have something to say, and often loudly, it's hard for anyone to find quiet. In a school packed with high-spirited adolescents, it's almost impossible. Even the school library, once a place of respectful silence, now turned Media Center, buzzes with activity. When my students write in class, they beg to listen to music through headphones and earbuds. They insist it calms and focuses them, and I believe them because they are simply unfamiliar with silence and its healing properties. I often tell my students, "You don't always have to fill the silence. Sometimes you can just enjoy it." Those are the times I think they wish *I* would just be silent.

The truth is that sometimes we as teachers are also guilty of trying to fill the silence, and sometimes that's precisely the reason class discussion goes nowhere. We've all had moments when what we hoped would be a period of fruitful discussion turns into a deadly stretch of empty air. We prompt and prod, rephrasing our questions and feigning more enthusiasm than we feel, but students simply stare at us (or more often at their desks, willing themselves to be invisible), until usually one brave and accommodating student ventures an answer, and, whether it's intelligent or not, we grasp it gratefully and move on, letting the potential for discussion die. Sometimes, if such a student doesn't come to our rescue, we grow reckless and resort to cold calling.

"Justin," I ask, "what do you think the connection is between Homer and a rose?"

Justin looks panicky, but he feels he has to say something. "Didn't he give Miss Emily a bunch of roses?" he says, though even he sounds unconvinced. But he's in it now. "Yeah, I think he did. Right?" He looks to his classmates for support. One or two nod, probably appreciating that Justin took one for the team.

Glad that students can't hear what goes on inside my head, I push on.

"I don't think you'll find that in the text. But there is a connection. Who has an idea?"

Eyes drop again to the desks. A few more motivated students flip madly through the pages of the story, hoping an answer will leap out at them.

This is excruciating, and meanwhile the clock is ticking down the minutes of the class period. I sigh and concede. "Could Homer be Miss Emily's rose? What do you think, Erik?"

Erik looks blank, but he's game. "Sure," he says with a shrug.

Buoyed, I move on.

"Who here has gotten flowers from someone, someone you liked, maybe for Valentine's Day or the prom?"

A few faces brighten. A few hands go up.

"Katie, what did you do with those flowers?'

She looks quizzical. "Threw 'em away, I guess. Or maybe my mom did."

Another roadblock, but I forge on.

"Did anyone keep them?" I ask hopefully.

"I did," Tina calls out. "I still have my prom flowers."

Now we're getting somewhere.

"And how did you keep them, Tina?" Even I can hear the note of desperate hope in my voice.

"I pressed them," she says boldly. "I put them in a big fat book and pressed them so I could keep . . ." Her eyes widen and she looks horrified. There's a sudden buzz in the classroom as the realization of the connection between Homer, a skeleton between the sheets, and the pressed flowers within the pages starts to spread from student to student.

"Yes!" I say triumphantly. "So, can we then agree that Homer is that pressed rose, a way for Miss Emily to hold on to love?"

The students nod vigorously—and begin to gather their materials. There are only a couple of minutes left in the period, and it seems "we" have found the answer. Clearly, the discussion is over for them. And what they really wanted to talk about anyway was how you'd keep a corpse.

Except this wasn't a discussion and, as the teacher, I am painfully aware of that. It stopped even having the potential for discussion the moment that Justin felt the need to answer the question and fill the silence with a response he knew was incorrect and unsupported by the text. However, as weak as his response was, for Justin it felt better than saying, "I don't know."

"I don't know" are dirty words in a classroom. We all know teachers who castigate students for saying those three utterly honest words. *I don't know* has somehow come to be taken as the lazy person's response. How often do teachers say, "Well, you must know something! Think about it!" or words to that effect. In fact, one often touted benefit of wait time is that it decreases the number of times student say, "I don't know" (Stahl 2). But why are we so disinclined to allow our students to speak this truth? How often, over the course of a day, do we ourselves answer questions with that simple, straightforward response? Why, then, in the classroom do we reject the plain reality of that response? Leah Hager Cohen, in her excellent book *I Don't Know: In Praise of Admitting Ignorance (Except When You Shouldn't)*, makes a convincing case for granting our students the permission to say, "I don't know," and for encouraging this response when it's a genuine one. When students don't feel free to admit ignorance, they either waste precious time creating phony answers that they hope will "pass" or, feeling inadequate, they drop out of the discussion entirely. Cohen writes, "People cheat when they are afraid. When there is no cost to being wrong or confessing ignorance, there is no reason to cheat or fake comprehension" (8). I think too about that student who wrote, "I sometimes flat out lie to avoid judgment for how I think or for the things I like. . . . I lie in conversation because it's so much less scary than being honest." Cheating, faking, and lying create a tremendous barrier, not just to class discussion but also to authentic learning and, in a wider sphere, to human connection. Cohen, whose book is a blend of research, personal narrative, and story, re-creates those instances we've all experienced when, embarrassed to admit our ignorance of a film, a news story, or a new hotspot our friends are discussing, we play along. We pretend we can follow the conversation instead of simply saying, "I don't know what you're talking about." We all know how uncomfortable our duplicitousness makes us feel, but we have all learned, perhaps from the very start of our education, how inadequate, how *stupid* we feel when we speak those three words, *I don't know*. But the consequences of such behavior go beyond discomfort. Playing along, pretending we know when we don't, hinders true human communication.

When, at the start of the school year, I talk about the importance of silence and that pause button in my classroom, I also talk about the importance of saying, "I don't know." I am adamant with my students that there is no shame in speaking those words. In fact, there's a certain integrity in speaking the truth by simply admitting one's ignorance. Students who struggle academically seem to understand this, and I think it makes them feel better about themselves and their academic challenges and therefore makes them more open to learning. It's my Honors students who recoil from this and resist speaking those three words. They feel they are *supposed* to know what the teacher asks them. They worry that an "I don't know" will cause their grade to fall. They feel constantly in competition with their classmates. And perhaps most significantly, their self-esteem is built upon their academic prowess. My job is to convince them that it shows true intelligence to admit to what one does not know. I remind them that saying "I don't know" isn't the same as saying "I don't care." Saying "I don't know" is an acknowledgment both of what one doesn't know and of what one is willing to learn, perhaps from others. Saying "I don't know" is a step forward to greater knowledge rather than a means of staying in place.

I frequently model the use of "I don't know" in the classroom, and it isn't a disingenuous act. Often when students ask questions, I *don't* know the answer. As a young teacher, that made me feel a failure, and I was sure it undermined my authority in the classroom. Years later I've come to realize that students appreciate the humility—and humanity—of a teacher who is willing to say "I don't know" rather than faking an answer. At the same time, it creates a teachable moment when I can show students how one goes about finding out what one doesn't know. Sometimes, if we're in search of a fact, I'll simply say, "Will someone please look that up on their phone?" Sometimes I'll direct them to an authority far more knowledgeable than I. "I think that's a question to ask your physics teacher," I'll say. And sometimes the question is one that doesn't have a correct answer but leads all of us to richer discussion. So when, in class discussion, a student tells me, "I don't know," I typically applaud their candor, accept their silence, and tell them that I trust they'll speak when they have something to say. As a teacher, I believe it's my responsibility to give students the space to be silent, and I think that freedom contributes positively to conversation as a whole.

The scene described earlier involving Justin, Erik, and Tina is a creative construct, a composite of classroom moments most of us are familiar with. But though the scene is fiction, the truths of it are corroborated by students' words. When I asked my students from different academic levels to freewite anonymously about conversation, both in the classroom and outside of it, they had a lot to say. Their words reflect the anxieties and conflicts they experience when it comes to classroom conversation.

> Our minds in school have been trained to just say what you think is correct and this removes all other ways of thinking.
>
> The difference between people talking in class and outside of class is the restriction of words. For example, students can't or aren't supposed to talk about whatever they want in the classroom. They are supposed to be only talking about what the teacher wants them to talk about.
>
> One thing about school is having to take part in a discussion for a grade. I never like those, and so do many people that don't like talking in class. It could be a topic I'm familiar with, it could even be about me, but when I'm forced to speak in front of others to discuss, I immediately forget everything and not make any sense while talking.
>
> I feel like in class people talk and kids do have conversations, but they are shut down by teachers because the "real" class needs to start. I think kids want to have a conversation but are less inclined when the topic becomes all educational. . . . That's probably why most teachers have us do independent work or use Chromebooks because we have a better chance of staying on task.
>
> I feel like in class we as students don't talk as much anymore. I feel like it's because teachers feel like we need to do something else. . . . Students feel afraid to talk.

These five comments express ideas that are repeated again and again in my students' reflections, and they echo the points I'm making in this chapter. The comments all relate to the idea that classroom conversation is hindered when students feel that words are, in effect, being put into their mouths. When students feel that the teacher controls the conversation, whether it be (1) by determining and limiting the focus of the discussion, (2) by requiring how students answer questions and move within the discussion, (3) by creating "discussion" aimed to culminate in the "right" answer—and perhaps a grade, or (4) by demanding participation in the discussion, students never become truly invested in the conversation and/or they lose interest in it.

To rectify these situations, I offer the following suggestions, understanding fully that none of these suggestions can always be implemented but believing that they should be utilized as much as possible:

1. Allow students the freedom to decide what they want to talk about. This doesn't mean a freewheeling discussion of subjects unrelated to the work students are doing. Rather, it means asking students what they want to know about the overall subject. What are the questions that popped into their heads as they read the assignment? Why are these things they want to know? What would they like to hear their classmates' opinions on? What matters to them? This can be done through a quick whole-class activity as students call out their questions and you put them on the board and then guide students though a discussion of these concerns. Experienced teachers know how to skillfully steer students from one idea to the next, and, in the process, they can make sure to emphasize those points and ideas that seem most significant and are ones that deserve extra attention. In doing so, they engage students in real conversation because the conversation is about things students really want to understand.

2. Clearly differentiate, not only for your students but also for yourself, the difference between questions that provoke discussion and those that seek a correct answer. There's nothing wrong with testing students' factual knowledge, but that's not the stuff of conversation. In real conversation, participants are eager to hear various ideas and opinions and welcome a steady exchange among participants. Generally, the pronouncement of a correct answer with the accompanying "You're right!" puts the brakes on conversation and ends the exchange. So, when you plan a class discussion, make sure that the intent of the activity is to generate a variety of ideas rather than the pursuit of the "right" answer.

3. Carefully weigh the positive and negative effects of grading a discussion, whether on the basis of content or process. While the threat of a grade may motivate more students to participate, it doesn't guarantee quality discussion, and in fact often leads to students speaking simply to get their required time in. Moreover, when you focus on trying to keep track of student participation, you're distracted from full participation in the discussion, which creates a situation atypical to real conversation. If we want our students to learn to talk to us and each other through a meaningful sharing of ideas, then we need to remove artificial structures that create pressure and inhibit true human communication.

4. Accept that class discussions won't always be smooth and structured, simply because they're the product of unique human personalities. If human beings in general are unpredictable and capricious, then teenagers are even more so, and any teacher who assumes they can routinely orchestrate fluid discussions among adolescents has a lot to learn. Some days students will speak and other days they won't. Some days students will stay on track, and other days their attention will wander far afield. And some days something seemingly benign will trigger an emotional spark that can send the conversation into overdrive and dangerous territory. You have to be mentally ready for all the ups and downs that are a part of any true human interaction, and some things you just can't predict or prepare for. But one thing you should avoid is depending too much on those students who dominate discussion. It's all too easy, especially when a discussion seems to stall, to defer to the perennial hand waver, but that invariably deters other students from joining the conversation. If certain students are perceived to always be "right," then others are naturally reluctant to offer divergent opinions. At the same time, those students who find it easier to sit back and avoid participation can abdicate responsibility and look to their classmates to keep the conversation moving.

5. Rethink what it means to have a "successful" discussion. Too often we measure success by the civility of the discussion, the number of students who speak, or the selection of points covered. We feel accomplished when we can say that 80 percent of our students spoke, that they stayed on track and took turns speaking, and that the key ideas we wanted them to understand were covered. Certainly all these things are integral to good discussion, but they don't define it. Good discussion is conversation that gets people thinking. It's the give-and-take of ideas that compels participants to see things in a way they haven't considered, that opens the door to others' perspectives, and that sometimes creates a feeling of discomfort. Good discussions are often messy and sometimes contentious, and they can't usually be summed up in the two minutes before the bell. A good discussion should end with students' minds bursting with ideas and with students still talking as the bell rings. When I hear students who are making their way out the door of Room C214 still debating the morality of Ethan Frome's choice to drive the sled into a tree, I feel that we might have had a very good discussion.

6. Last, and perhaps most importantly, remember that class conversation is not a supplement to your teaching but is in fact at the heart of real teaching and real learning. Too often teachers regard class discussion as something

"extra," an activity that complements and enhances the "real teaching." Students tend to think the same. We hear that from the student who writes about a stalled discussion and says, "and the teacher sits in silence for a painful minute until they finally say something to wrap it up and continue teaching." There's an unspoken idea that if the discussion doesn't work, then we go back to "real" teaching, whether that be via lectures or worksheets or writing assignments. The truth is, what students learn in discussion, *real* discussion, can't be replicated via any other teaching method because in discussion they learn that knowledge is rarely absolute. They learn that one must wrestle with ideas, one's own and those of others, to discover that which goes beyond the factual. They learn to clearly articulate their beliefs and support their opinions, and to truly *hear* the beliefs and opinions of others. And they learn that all of this is risky because all of this is real, and that is what makes true learning exhilarating

I end this chapter by returning to the Stan Getz quote that opened it: "As far as playing jazz, no other art form, other than conversation, can give the satisfaction of spontaneous interaction." So little in education is spontaneous these days. But when it comes to discussion, it's up to us as teachers to celebrate spontaneity and to welcome the sound of words that flow freely from of our students' mouths.

6

"We Need to Talk": Navigating Difficult Conversations

Be brave enough to start a conversation that matters.

—Margaret Wheatley

We speak often these days of living in a brave new world, one rich with change and challenges that, a generation ago, we could likely not have envisioned. My students cannot conceive of a world without technology, nor can they imagine one without disease, school shootings, political divisiveness, and social injustice. They look ahead and wonder how they will find economic stability, save the planet, raise their children, and end the violence. And they feel very alone. Twenge describes this generation:

> In the three years I've spent working on this book . . . I've realized this: iGen'ers are scared, maybe even terrified. Growing up slowly, raised to value safety, and frightened by the implications of income inequality, they have come to adolescence in a time when their primary social activity is staring at a small rectangular screen that can like them or reject them. The devices they hold in their hands have both extended their childhoods and isolated them from true human interaction. As a result, they are both the physically safest generation and the most mentally fragile. They are more focused on work and more realistic than Millennials, grasping the certainty that they'll need to fight hard to make it. They're exquisitely tolerant and have brought a new awareness of equality, mental health, and LGBT rights, leaving behind traditional structures such as religion. iGen'ers have a solid basis for success, with their practical nature and their inherent caution. If they can shake themselves free of the constant clutch of their phones and shrug off the heavy cloak of their fear, they can still fly. (312–13)

This description was written in 2017, before COVID-19 rendered our students more isolated, more fearful, and more dependent than ever on their phones and screens. It was written before the deepest impact of the profound political divide in America showed itself in so many ways, leaving young people struggling to find their footing and their voice in a world where differences of opinion are rancorous and often dangerous. The young people we meet in our classrooms today are, I think, iGen'ers in the extreme, and that means that we as teachers must challenge them in ways that may make them—and us—uncomfortable if ever, as Twenge suggests, we want them to fly.

Difficult conversations are, well, difficult. Whether with a friend or colleague, with a parent or spouse, or with thirty adolescents, a conversation that touches on controversial issues and raw nerves is a test of courage and diplomacy. Difficult conversations demand a deep breath, a squaring of the shoulders, and a mental step forward. How much easier, then, to avoid such conversations in classrooms where so many lives intersect and where disagreement and dissent are guaranteed. In some school systems, teachers are encouraged to avoid such exchanges in order to create classrooms that are "safe," in the worst sense of the word. Yes, classrooms need to be safe, but they need to be safe spaces where students can express their opinions, explore their beliefs, challenge their opponents respectfully, and ultimately learn the meaning of tolerance.

Most of our students have grown up in a world where civil conversation, particularly in the public sphere, is practically nonexistent. They hear those in power lambaste one another with lies and invectives. Protests are filled with violence and vitriol. Arguments are supported by spurious "facts" and met with closed minds. Many students have learned to choose sides, stand firm, and block their ears so as not to be swayed by the shouting of the "other side," while they strive to make their own voices even more strident. Meanwhile, some of them have learned to step back, drop out, and stay "safe" in a bubble of created apathy.

The classroom, then, may be the last bastion of civil conversation, which puts an enormous responsibility on us as educators. If we don't allow our students the safety, the space, and the opportunity to engage in difficult conversations, we are doing them an immense disservice, and I question whether it's one that can ever be remediated. The lucky students may go off to college where meaningful conversation is generally fostered and furthered, but for many of our students, the end of senior year signals entry into the workforce and adulthood, and into a world where sides are drawn and positions solidified, a world where tolerance is too often missing.

There are far too many hot button issues to list them all here, but as teachers we know them well (and sometimes we're surprised by issues that suddenly become charged). Racial prejudice and stereotyping, religious freedom, abortion, gun control, immigration, LGBTQ+ rights, climate change, social stratification, political ideologies . . . the divides are vast and passion on all sides high. How do we conduct classroom conversations that give students the opportunity to explore and express their feelings on these sorts of issues while maintaining an engaged and respectful interaction among them?

I offer here my own approach, but at the end of this chapter, I include a list of excellent resources on the topic of difficult conversations, and I highly encourage you to review this material. These groups, including Learning for Justice and Facing History and Ourselves, have as a goal the creation of a just, equitable, and tolerant world, and their material is extremely valuable for negotiating hard conversations. I readily admit to using and adapting some of these resources in my handling of difficult classroom conversations, so much so that I honestly don't know what to attribute to whom, and certainly many techniques extend beyond any one source. My intent in focusing here on specific approaches I use is to highlight key responsibilities of the teacher who wants to create a classroom space where difficult conversations can become easier. It's important, however, to emphasize that every teacher must consider carefully their own level of comfort. If you are tense, awkward, or edgy, that will be conveyed to students and hinder meaningful discussion. Though I firmly believe that we have a responsibility to open our classrooms to these hard conversations, teachers who feel uncomfortable doing so need to approach this slowly in order to develop their own sense of ease and confidence.

Ground Rules

I always begin the school year with that one rule: "Be nice to each other." To me, that says it all, but I know it is not always enough when tempers flare and fierce and fiery words begin to fly about the classroom. So early on in the year (hopefully before I can be surprised by an impassioned discussion I didn't expect!), I ask my students to talk in groups of three or four about those things that make a good discussion. Invariably, they prove to me that though they may not always *have* good discussions, they do know what goes into them. When these small-group conversations have ended, I invite students up to the board to write short phrases that for them define the qualities of a good discussion. I encourage them to note what other students write and, if their group has a similar idea, to simply put a check mark next to that quality.

They fill the board quickly: *Everyone doesn't talk at once. Nobody dominates. Everyone who wants to can talk. People listen to each other. The topic is interesting. The teacher doesn't talk all the time. The teacher lets us talk. No swearing. No name calling. No bullying. You don't have to talk if you don't want to. Nobody leaves mad.* What they write is always wise and well considered, but they're quick to recognize that these expectations aren't always met when a discussion blooms. So, as a class, we talk about the problems we've all experienced in discussions, and then we draw up a list of ground rules that will help guide us when we're caught up in the momentum of a classroom conversation. I don't devise one standard list of rules, because I want these guidelines to arise from my students, the soon-to-be participants in discussion. Instead, I do this exercise with each individual class, and, though of course the final list of rules each class comes up with is similar, I often can tell fairly quickly what each particular group of students has experienced previously in class discussions and what makes them wary. My Honors-level students generally focus on the need to be heard; they hint at a fear of not getting their moment in the spotlight. Students at a lower academic level often seem concerned about angry outbursts and the potential for a wild free-for-all. Quiet groups emphasize permission to not engage in the discussion, while more boisterous classes want to talk about how many times each person can talk—and how to quiet the teacher. For me what's important is that students understand their responsibility to engage in productive discussion and that they have together created a general list of ground rules to make that happen. These ground rules are ones that we can then refer back to when, in the course of a discussion, things start to spin out of control.

Employing the Ground Rules: Techniques for Facilitating Difficult Conversations

Creating Space

And things do spin out of control. Suddenly a discussion of economic inequality, such as might evolve from reading Gloria Naylor's "Kiswana Browne," becomes a shouting match as Braden decries any sort of government assistance for those in need, while Jess attacks him in increasingly insulting terms for being rich and elitist and not understanding anything about poverty. Their classmates sit back, seeming to enjoy the altercation. Meanwhile, I know that Michelle and her father lived for a time in their car, and I can see that she's staring down at her desk, probably wishing she could just disappear. This is when I as the teacher have to step in, not to stop the discussion but to defuse it long enough to return it to a productive activity, and I do this based on the ground rules these very same students created.

I have some choices here, depending on the intensity of the exchange and what I know about this particular group of students. I can start by employing that pause button and a simple "time out" strategy. "Remember," I can say, "how we all decided that everyone gets to speak and no one gets to dominate? Let's take a deep breath and just think about that for a couple of minutes, and then continue this discussion." Though I can't control what students are thinking, I'm adamant that they sit silently for a minute or two, and this pause often is enough to calm the heightening tensions and end the Braden versus Jess show. I then might ask, "So who else has something to contribute on either side, or a new point we haven't talked about?"—and that invitation welcomes new speakers and ideas into the conversation.

Sometimes, however, more than a breath and a pause are needed to de-escalate the divisions. Sometimes beliefs and opinions are so ingrained that students are virtually incapable of stepping back enough to separate their emotional reaction from their intellectual response. In these instances, students need more time to process their thoughts and perhaps recalculate their emotional meters. If this is the situation, I ask students to write for five to ten minutes, both about the topic we're discussing and the way they're feeling. This written reflection works in a number of ways. First, it typically slows the angry flow of words that verbal speech allows—and, at least temporarily, it removes the audience for whom those angry words were intended. Second, it gives each student the chance to reassess their feelings in a nonthreatening arena. In this written piece, they don't have to defend their beliefs against those on the other side but instead simply state their thoughts clearly and calmly, and, as a result, they are sometimes more willing to see the potential for compromise. Last, if the timing's right and this activity takes place close to the end of the period, I can take these pieces home in order to see more clearly what's going on in my students' heads—and hearts. I can correct patently incorrect information, and sometimes I can see points of connection and compromise that may have escaped the speakers. This material helps me facilitate further and better discussion the next time we meet.

Learning to Listen

Sometimes there are just so many passionate voices involved in a discussion that no one hears what anyone else is trying to say. This is the time to remind students of the importance of listening to each other. Listening sounds like a simple skill; you sit there quietly and hear another person speak. If only it were that easy. These days, we don't do a lot of listening to one another. And if you need proof of that, consider this. When I googled "how to listen," the Google search function offered me three specific options: "how to listen to podcasts," "how to listen to music offline," and "how to listen to Spotify offline." Clearly, "how to listen to other people in real life" is an outdated practice! I tell my students that, above all else, the ability to truly listen demands an open mind. I'm certain we can all think of situations when we've vehemently declared we *are* listening. Perhaps a spouse aired concerns about the division of household labor, or a ninth grader's parent wanted to explain why she was sure her son was gifted, or a neighbor expressed a questionable political view. In these cases, I'm sure we all heard the speaker's words—and were quite able to repeat them back when righteously denouncing what we heard. But real listening demands that the listener "suspend" their own views and beliefs long enough to openly welcome the speaker's words, to calmly process those words, and to seek further clarification and understanding.

In "What Great Listeners Actually Do," Jack Zenger and Joseph Folkman challenge some of the more traditional beliefs about listening. As children (and I suspect as students), we were likely taught that listening meant being silent and attentive, ignoring other distractions, and perhaps offering a nod or a murmur to show we were in fact paying attention. The idea is that listeners listen while speakers speak. Zenger and Folkman, however, offer a different model, one based on research done for the business community and the training of managers, but one that seems equally appropriate for good classroom listening. In particular, they offer two conclusions that teachers would do well to promote in their classrooms:

> Good listening is much more than being silent while the other person talks. To the contrary, people perceive the best listeners to be those who periodically ask questions that promote discovery and insight. . . . Sitting there silently nodding does not provide sure evidence that a person is listening, but asking a good question tells the speaker the listener has not only heard what was said, but that they comprehended it well enough to want additional information. Good listening was consistently seen as a two-way dialog, rather than a one-way "speaker vs hearer" interaction. (Zenger and Folkman)

Consider this in terms of classroom dynamics. When we demand that students sit silently while someone voices an opinion, we're not really encouraging give-and-take but actually allowing students the time to "plan their attack" while one student is speaking. In "real life"—life outside the classroom—we show that we are truly listening when we interrupt to ask for clarification or further explanation. This is different, of course, from interrupting simply to stop the speaker or to steal the stage, and students need to be taught the difference, but it's an important practice, and it makes for real conversation rather than angry argument. To test that this is going on in my classroom, I sometimes jump in as a student is speaking to ask the class what questions they have for the speaker or what they need to know more about in order to fully understand what's been said. When I do this and they all look at me blankly, I know they weren't really listening, and this becomes a teachable moment.

In another of their other findings, Zenger and Folkman explain that

> good listening included interactions that build a person's self-esteem. The best listeners made the conversation a positive experience for the other party, which doesn't happen when the listener is passive (or, for that matter, critical!). Good listeners made the other person feel supported and conveyed confidence in them. Good listening was characterized by the creation of a safe environment in which issues and difference could be discussed openly.

When I first read this, I thought, hmmm, isn't that the *teacher's* role? Don't we consider it our responsibility to create a positive environment and to bolster each student's confidence as a speaker? Only on deeper reflection did I realize that this is actually a responsibility I can—and should—pass on to my students. Students, and too often adults, are frequently all too ready to go on the attack to refute a speaker's words. This tactic creates not conversation but competition, and it demonstrates a participant's inability or refusal to listen and to consider another side. If we can begin to train students to respectfully acknowledge and explore the points they hear, even when discussion grows heated, then we have taught them not only a measure of civility but also a means of honestly assessing the validity of their views.

Studies done by David Broockman and Joshua Kalla demonstrate a powerful reason to promote this sort of listening. Broockman and Kalla's work indicates that "when it comes to changing someone's feelings about issues[,] . . . data are less compelling than human stories. Listening is more powerful than just talking. Accepting the other person, even if their ideas feel offensive, may open the door to constructive dialogue" (Lempinen). Their fieldwork, done in the area of political persuasion, shows the success of what is termed *deep canvassing*. This approach is "based on asking sensitive questions, listening to the answers with sincere interest and then asking more questions" (Lempinen). Canvassers, who often met with opposition in their support of immigration and transgender rights, engaged participants in conversation and the exchange of stories and discovered that this personal interaction had a positive impact that the mere recitation of facts did not. Broockman and Kalla's field experiments demonstrated that when door-to-door canvassers both listened to and shared stories with those in opposition, there was a change in attitude. Broockman explains, "'It's really hard to change people's minds. . . . When we talk about persuasion, we talk so much about how to make the most effective arguments, the most effective talking points. But we don't talk so much about how to be a good listener, or about how to make people comfortable in talking to you and hearing from you'" (qtd. in Lempinen).

In connection with this is the work of Peter T. Coleman, a professor of psychology at Columbia University and director of the Morton Deutsch International Center for Cooperation and Conflict Resolution. Coleman reflects on the way we approach opposing ideas and explains the critical difference between dialogue and debate:

> The term "dialogue" is often employed to describe the process of talking over our differences; however, most Americans don't dialogue—they automatically resort to debate. This is because we are highly socialized to debate through learning it in school, by watching legal proceedings (all 456 episodes of "Law and Order"), or when following political campaigns. Debate also feels like a more fitting response to political differences when emotions run high—a chance to defend yourself and intellectually challenge and defeat the other.
>
> But, there is a profound difference between debate and dialogue. Debate involves a closed, strategic form of persuasion aimed at winning an argument. It involves making a case for your side, then listening attentively to the other side to identify flaws in their logic that you can use against them.
>
> Dialogue is the opposite. It involves a process of opening, sharing and discovery, similar to what is often seen in AA meetings. It usually requires a carefully facilitated process where the participants share personal stories about their own experiences and often learn new things about themselves, the others and the issues under discussion. (Coleman)

These ideas have, I think, significant implications for the classroom. We may not be in the business of changing people's minds, but we are certainly working to open those minds. When students confront one another in the classroom, we often think the best arguments are those based on facts and figures and a carefully constructed argument. I know I have often praised students for the hard data they bring to a discussion. This material is important, as we all want students to learn from the conversations they share. But, if we want our students to develop the ability to participate in civil and constructive discussion, then I think we need to teach them to approach such a discussion with empathy and openness, and that is born of listening, especially when the speaker shares the personal experiences that contribute to their beliefs. If we want our students to be better at narrowing and perhaps even crossing the many divides that exist in our country today, we need to teach them to hear all sides and to fully understand that the words they hear, even when such words seem dreadful or dangerous, spring from human experience and vulnerability. We must teach our students to speak candidly, sharing that which has shaped their beliefs, and to listen intently, searching for true understanding. Ultimately, we need to trust that a commitment to both activities will result in authentic human connection—and perhaps even accord.

Encouraging Empathy

My students struggle with the idea of empathy. They confuse it with apathy, consider it synonymous with sympathy, and generally find the whole idea of it bothersome. I try to be empathetic, but, quite honestly, I bristle when they dismiss the importance of empathy. Then I have to remind myself that this disinterest in being deeply interested in others isn't a new phenomenon. Indeed, in his 2006 address to Northwestern University graduates, then Senator Barack Obama spoke of the "empathy deficit": "The world doesn't just revolve around you. There's a lot of talk in this country about the federal deficit. But I think we should talk more about our empathy deficit—the ability to put ourselves in someone else's shoes; to see the world through those who are different from us—the child who's hungry, the laid-off steelworker, the immigrant woman cleaning your dorm room."

Sara Konrath, associate professor of philanthropic studies at Indiana University and director of the Interdisciplinary Program on Empathy and Altruism Research, describes two kinds of empathy: "Empathy is both imagining other people's perspectives and their world's cognitive type of empathy, and it's also caring, compassion and concern for others, that emotional empathy" ("Speaking of Psychology"). I would hope that as teachers we would strive to help our students develop both, but it's perhaps the former that the consistent practice of conversation in the classroom best addresses. If we can help our students develop the ability to fully imagine another's perspective, to in effect know what it's like to be them, this would be an extraordinary step forward in healing the divisions that are so prevalent in our society.

Konrath's research shows a major decline in empathy among students in the years from 1979 to 2009 ("Speaking of Psychology"), while studies of young people in the last decade are still ongoing. Certainly, young people in recent years have demonstrated a positive civic involvement in their fight for equality, their concern about the environment, and their overall activism, all of which speaks to their capacity for empathy. But I don't always see such empathy in my students' everyday interactions in the classroom or on their screens, and I worry about their ability to maintain a sense of empathy when they enter the adult world, with its focus on individual success. It's when I listen to them talk to each other in serious classroom conversations that I hear the strongest and most hopeful demonstrations of empathy, and this is something I want to nurture.

In *Reclaiming Conversation*, Sherry Turkle describes her work as a consultant at a middle school in upstate New York in 2013:

> Time with people teaches children how to be in a relationship, beginning with the ability to have a conversation. . . . As the Holbrooke middle schoolers began to spend more time texting, they lost practice in face-to-face talk. That means lost practice in the empathic arts—learning to make eye contact, to listen, to attend to others. Conversation is on the path toward the experience of intimacy, community, and communion. Reclaiming conversation is a step toward reclaiming our most fundamental human values. (7)

The question is, how do we teach the "empathic arts"? Providing continued opportunities for meaningful conversation is vital, but even when the occasion presents itself, it isn't always easy for adolescents to put themselves in someone else's shoes—or for someone to display the shoes they are wearing. As a group, adolescents are self-conscious and fearful of judgment and are reluctant to reveal the struggles they are facing. Through their vast experience with social media, they have learned skills that allow them to mask whatever they choose not to reveal. But if classroom conversations are to have real depth and meaning and ultimately have an impact on our students, we want them to tackle difficult issues such as poverty, injustice, mental health, discrimination, and abuse, and we need them to be candid about their own experiences and beliefs. We want students to develop empathy for those who are facing such issues, and we want them to understand that we are all vulnerable simply because we are all human.

As English teachers, we have an extraordinary "tool" to help our students develop empathy. That tool is the literature we teach. For the reader, literature opens the door to worlds where one might find connection and comfort—or to an entirely new way of being. For the teacher, literature creates an entryway into ideas that we want our students to explore, and when those ideas are somewhat uncomfortable, literature offers a bit of distance, allowing students to reflect through the characters and their situations before they speak for themselves. For all of us, literature offers the opportunity for connection:

> What other activity so deftly balances undistracted isolation and engaged social interaction? In one respect, reading first requires the self, stripped bare to one's consciousness in the face of another's narrative, to confront a text. (Kafka called reading "an axe for the frozen sea within us.") In another respect, reading pulls us out of ourselves into various communities of thought, venues in which empathy

> and interpretation converge at a single point of reference. Anyone who has ever shared enthusiasm for a book understands Emerson's definition of friendship as a phenomenon where you and another person "see the same truth." And even if the interpretations that come from isolated inquiry end up clashing, George Eliot's statement that reading is "a mode of amplifying experience and extending our contact with our fellow men" still holds true. (McWilliams)

Though some teachers might prefer to back away from works such as *To Kill a Mockingbird*, *The Adventures of Huckleberry Finn*, *The Bluest Eye*, or *Night*, or more contemporary choices such as *Thirteen Reasons Why*, *Persepolis*, or *The Absolutely True Diary of a Part-Time Indian*, the reality is that these challenging—and sometimes challenged—books give students and teachers alike a safe place to begin the hard conversations we need to have. Through thoughtful classroom discussion, students can confront important societal issues as well as their own biases and prejudices and, in the process, work toward a sense of empathy. In her interview with the American Psychological Association, Konrath describes the power that fiction has in the creation of empathy:

> Overall, the research is finding that just reading in general is helpful, but fiction in particular because it allows us to imagine other people's lives. Oftentimes in fiction, you're getting a window into what's going on in someone's mind. You can almost see the world through their eyes and practice what it might be like to be another person. That person could be somebody really, really different.
>
> It can be a different gender, or political affiliation, or ethnicity, or culture. You just get to live all these different lives and to stay close to people you might not encounter in your everyday life from the inside perspective. ("Speaking of Psychology")

I am well aware that many teachers are faced with a prescribed curriculum, and I know that I'm lucky in having quite a bit of discretion in the books I choose for my students to read. But I would be hard pressed to imagine any well-regarded piece of literature that didn't offer students a "window" into someone's else world. This, however, clearly speaks to why it's important that we offer our students a diverse selection of reading materials, and that we make certain that our students don't experience a "white only" world in their reading.

My own selections are almost always dependent on what I think a particular novel, short story, play, or poem can offer my students in terms of their growing understanding of others, oftentimes in conjunction with relevant issues in society. I don't ignore the content and quality of the work, but I want my students to explore ideas that reach beyond the plot and page. So yes, Raymond

Carver's short story "Little Things" is a prime example of the minimalist style of writing, but we read it because I want my students to consider what life is like on the edge of poverty, and Carver is the voice of that segment of society. And yes, *Fences* is a brilliant play that helped to cement August Wilson's place in the American theater canon, but I want my students to understand how the struggle for Civil Rights not only changed society as a whole but also had a deeply personal impact on African American families as they faced change. And yes, *The Things They Carried* by Tim O'Brien is a remarkable picture of the Vietnam War, but I want my students to recognize that war isn't only about countries or ideologies but about individuals who will carry the impact of their experience long after a peace treaty is signed. Each of these works has sparked stimulating conversation directly related to the literature itself (Did they really kill the baby? Why does Rose agree to raise the child Troy fathered outside of their marriage? Who or what is responsible for Ted Lavender's death?), but more important, each has opened the door to conversation about what it is that make us human. Each provokes important questions. What is our responsibility to others? What drives us to violence? To whom do we owe our lives? How do we recover from trauma? What gives life meaning? I believe these difficult questions are vitally important for adolescents to explore if they are to develop their own personal belief systems and become adults who can cooperate in and contribute to society as a whole. In the best moments, the exploration that starts with literature allows them to feel safe enough to begin to share their own stories, and that is when real empathy is born.

"I like this guy," Max announces, three stories in on the unit on Raymond Carver and after much class conversation about Carver's characters and the struggles they face to survive, physically and emotionally. Max is a school choice student with a background and home situation that make him something of an anomaly and an outsider to most of my students. As products of affluent homes and seemingly prosperous lives, they can sometimes manifest too much entitlement and too little empathy.

"Me too," I tell him. "I like his honesty. I like that he just tells it like it is. How about you?"

Max shrugs. "I don't know. It's just that he gets it."

The other students are listening, or at least they're sitting quietly, looking attentive.

"Gets what?" I probe.

Max just sits there for minute. His jaw tightens, and I wonder if I should rescue him and move on. But it seems like a moment when—

"He gets it. What it's like not to have anything. Not just money. Anything. You know, man," he pauses, and then laughs in a way that we all know isn't funny, "like me."

He doesn't say anything else, and I know intuitively that it's not my place to push him further. But the kids get it. They're aware that they have witnessed a moment of vulnerability, or what Carver might describe as a moment of grace. And I think that in that moment, they understand what it means to be someone other than themselves, and I think that by reading Carver, Max has also come to understand that it's fine to be exactly who he is. In Carver's world, there are few happy endings, but there are these moments when people find and feel a connection to one another. When they experience empathy. When they "get it." This is one such moment.

And there are others. My sophomores read "Firebug," a story by Katie Cortese, published in 2012 and included in her 2018 collection *Make Way for Her*. The story describes a teenage girl, Jessica, who struggles with pyrokinesis. Her attempts to control her often uncontrollable ability to set things on fire set her apart from her peers and leave her feeling isolated. Told in the second person, the story draws readers in, making them feel Jessica's frustration and fear as she attempts to cope with her differences. As a class, we first talk about the story as an example of magical realism, but I'm hoping someone will take it to a deeper level. What I'm not expecting is that the someone will be Jenny, a young woman who faces her own challenges with Asperger's and does seem somewhat "apart" from her classmates. I see her hand hovering over her desk.

"Jenny," I say, "do you have some ideas about the story?"

She hesitates, and her words stop and start and detour a bit as is her way, but then she says firmly, "So I think it's a metaphor."

"Interesting idea," I say. "Can you talk about that? How might it work as a metaphor?"

And so she begins to speak. I don't have a recording of that day, and I would be doing Jenny an injustice to try to re-create her moving and eloquent explanation of how pyrokinesis represents those things that make some of us different, in her own case Asperger's. I have rarely heard her speak so well or so openly, perhaps finding in the experiences of Jessica the courage to confront the twenty-five classmates around her with her own loneliness. She explains to them what it means to have Asperger's, and her words are both poignant and informative. When she finishes, there's a short silence, and then suddenly one . . . two . . . three . . . other students begin to speak about their own sense of isolation. To be Asian in a school of predominantly white students, to be gay and hiding it at home, to suffer from depression so severe that leads to hospitalization. . . . Because of

Jenny (and Jessica), these students are now willing to let others into their world, and they enter without hesitation, asking questions and open to understanding. Whether any of these students will ever remember much about "Firebug" itself, I don't know, but I do know they will remember Jenny's bravery, and I feel certain that conversation will have a positive effect on the way they interact with those they perceive as different. That is the power of empathy and the reason we as teachers must do all we can to cultivate it in our classrooms, through the material we choose to teach and the conversations we encourage.

So not all difficult conversations are confrontational. Some help us forge connections and some help us through the pain and turmoil we all face. Sometimes we have these conversations in the hope that, through shared words, we can find a way to make sense of reality, particularly when the reality is horrifying. I suspect we have all been called on to teach our way through a deeply difficult moment—9/11, the Stoneman Douglas shootings, the killing of Trayvon Martin, a student suicide; the list is long. There are things that happen in the world that are infinitely more important than the material on our syllabi, and so we pause the curriculum to try to help our students make sense of life at these moments. In these instances, even when students are often united in their feelings, we can find ourselves engaged in difficult conversations because of the intense emotion they elicit. These are times when students often lash out, attacking all in a group because of the actions of one, making sweeping generalizations in their attempt to control what is out of their control, or simply railing against what they see as the unfairness of life. We want them to talk and to find solace in a classroom community that shares their pain, but we need to make sure the conversation we have doesn't foster a mob mentality or fuel flames of wanton anger in reaction to pain and loss. I also want students to feel empathy for those most closely involved and to understand that a national tragedy is also, for some, a very personal heartbreak and loss.

This is another time when literature can help shape the conversation. One of the most effective approaches I've found is through the use of poetry. When tragedy strikes and we have to make quick decisions about how to address that tragedy in our classroom, poetry is easily accessible and often able to offer perspective and comfort. This was made especially clear to me in the early days of the pandemic when school suddenly closed, leaving all of us grappling with how to cope and, as teachers, with how to teach. The Academy of American Poets, through its website (https://poets.org), quickly came to the aid of teachers by offering extensive teaching materials and resources especially focused on helping to engage students who were now suddenly far away from us. What I most appreciated at that time was the collection of "shelter in" poems, including

Kay Ryan's "Patience," Joy Harjo's "Perhaps the World Ends Here," and Juan Felipe Herrera's "Social Distancing," that, along with accompanying activities, allowed my students to process the isolation they were feeling via poetry. Occasionally as an assignment I would ask students to choose a poem from the suggested lists that had meaning for them and read it with someone in their home or someone they could talk to either by phone or computer. I stressed the need to *talk* to this other person, to discuss the poem in detail, and to consider how it related to their own immediate experience, and I asked them to take time to think deeply about the conversation that resulted. At that time, we weren't able to meet virtually as a class to talk about these poems or about how both the poetry and the sharing of it impacted their stay-at-home experience, but their written reflections assured me that they were benefiting from both the beauty of poetry and the opportunity to share it with others. That literary connection lessened the loneliness and perhaps gave them and their conversational partners a broader perspective on the situation we all found ourselves in, as well as a stronger sense of empathy.

The Academy of American Poets also takes an active role in promoting social justice through the use of poetry, and the poems featured can be effectively used to promote conversation on a wide variety of social concerns. Teachers can go to https://poets.org/materials-teachers to search for poems on a particular topic to find ready material. Long before Amanda Gorman became well known in 2021 as the youngest inaugural poet, her poem "In This Place (An American Lyric)" spoke to my students. Classroom activities offered on the website include a video of Gorman reading the poem, as well as suggestions for connecting this poem to Martin Luther King Jr.'s "I Have a Dream" speech (Holzer). The poem addresses contemporary events and the inequality evident throughout our society. This poem and others like it give students the opportunity to first enter into conversations about topics such as racial injustice with the distance that literature allows and, in the process, establish the confidence to then explore these controversial issues on a more personal level with one another.

Establishing an End

As most of us know from personal experience, it can be hard to end a difficult conversation—or at least to end it well. We can find our words going in circles, tension rising, with no resolution in sight (save perhaps the slamming of a door). Teachers and students in a classroom, like boxers in a ring, are in a sense fortunate in that the sound of a bell signals the end of a "round," giving opponents time to recuperate and regroup. In *We Need to Talk*, Celeste Headlee names "five key strategies that help facilitate a productive discussion. They are: be curious, check your bias, show respect, stay the course, and end well" (63). We teachers need to be particularly cognizant of that last strategy.

Discussions shouldn't have winners and losers; they are not debates. Class discussions, even the most difficult, should be an arena for the airing of ideas. Participants should feel free to express their honest opinions and be willing to elaborate on and explain their ideas when asked. Everyone should carefully process and consider all that they hear, but no one should feel pressured to change their mind (though I admit there are times when I fervently wish that a student who expresses views that are narrow-minded at best could be persuaded otherwise). Most important, when the difficult discussion ends and students walk out the door of my classroom, I want to know that (1) they are all right and (2) they will be all right.

By this I mean, foremost, that I don't want anyone to leave hurt or angry. Students can certainly leave the room holding widely disparate views and weary from energetic exchanges, but no one should feel hurt, ostracized, or irate because of the views they expressed or heard. There are times during these intense conversations when I can tell instantly that someone has been wounded by another student's words, and in those cases I ask for an apology. If a student has been outwardly and intentionally rude, calling a classmate stupid or worse or attacking them unfairly, then I want that apology to happen immediately in the context of the class discussion. All students need to be aware that such behavior won't be tolerated. I expect that apology to be sincere. No one needs to apologize for their views, but students do need to express regret when they fail to communicate those views civilly.

Occasionally an apology is better discussed and delivered privately. I've seen students put up a brave front when someone hurts them, and I'm not sure I would be helping the situation by jumping in to demand a public apology. Sometimes pride is in itself an effective balm. But in those instances, I talk to both students privately, to the offender to express my concerns over their behavior and to the offended to see how they would like me to handle the situation. Sometimes both agree that they need to talk things out, and other times they assure me things are better left alone. In any case, these types of situations are important to talk about, not only with the individual students but also with the class as a whole in order to emphasize the need for civil discourse and attention to the established ground rules for discussion.

The issue of "Will they be all right?" is a concern somewhat out of my control but of which I need to be aware. I don't want students leaving my classroom with tempers high and ready to do battle. I don't want conflicts to spill out into the hallways or the cafeteria and, should it appear that could happen, I believe it's my responsibility to seriously de-escalate the situation. If such a situation involves only a couple of students, then I hold back those students and talk them down, aiming not only to calm them but also to extract a promise not to take their opposing views further. Often, just the fact that they know I'm aware of the tension and am concerned about it is enough to end it. But if the tension involves a portion of the class, I rely on one of the following techniques.

Overall, it's much more likely that students will leave a passionate discussion with positive feelings if the teacher is careful to allow time for debriefing. Though it's tempting to let an animated discussion run right up to the bell, it's not a wise idea, as students need time to calmly process all that they've heard and feel. I know teachers who have found success with a "wrap up" kind of conversation in which students individually share their feelings about the conversation. Teachers need to be careful, however, that this doesn't lapse back into continued discussion rather than simply serving as a sort of check-in.

While verbal debriefing can be effective, it's close to impossible to successfully sum up all that transpires in a spirited discussion in a few minutes. I find it more beneficial to have students write about what they are thinking and feeling about the discussion, and I assure them that I will read these pieces before the next time we meet. Putting emotion into written words is one of the best ways of managing it. Moreover, this practice allows *every* student the chance to "speak their piece" without interruption, knowing that I will be an audience for their words. I hope too that putting their thoughts into written words reminds students that discussion is an intellectual pursuit, not warfare. Although I don't require that students respond to specific questions, I put some on the board as suggestions to focus their writing. These questions might include:

What did you hear that you are in firm agreement with—and why?

What did you hear that you find difficult to agree with—and why?

What did you hear that surprised you?

What would you like to ask more questions about?

Is there anything you wish you had said, but didn't? Why didn't you say this?

Is there anything you wish you hadn't said, but did? Why do you feel this way?

Overall, how did this conversation make you feel?

What will you take away or remember from this conversation?

Reflections that explore these kinds of questions help me to understand how my students processed and interpreted the discussion and can greatly contribute to effective follow-up to that discussion. A next day follow-up, especially when the conversation has been hard and heated, is vital. Though it can be tempting to simply let a difficult conversation fade away, that negates the importance of that discussion, and it can lead to unresolved and sometimes festering feelings.

Generally, at the very end of the period, I offer my own brief summary of the discussion, a kind of "this is what I heard" review. This can help students remember what was said and can sometimes allow them to see where even those in conflict might find points of agreement. I also explain where I expect the class and the conversation to go from here, and I encourage students to consider how all the ideas expressed relate to their overall learning. It's essential that students know that a discussion isn't just a casual classroom activity but rather an integral part of their learning experience, and that the material that comes out of it is as important as anything they get from the pages of a textbook. I let them know that though we may not spend the entire next class period continuing the discussion, we will take time then to share some last thoughts.

Two Voices, Two Views

Although this is a book on conversation, speaking and writing naturally intersect, and one can benefit the other, a topic I address in Chapter 7. But a specific writing activity that I have found to be an effective accompaniment when attempting to navigate difficult conversations is the two-voice poem. Two-voice poems are much like dialogues and are written for two speakers. Each speaker's ideas are presented in a separate column, and speakers go back and forth, as in conversation, when presenting the entire poem. Typically, some lines connect the speakers, and those are lines that the two read together. Such lines appear in the middle of the page or on the same line in each column. In style and design, then, these poems, with their two distinct voices, are particularly well suited for the expression of conflicting viewpoints and can help students who are on opposite sides of an issue find common ground.

Many websites offer material on two-voice poetry, as a Google search will show. Inspired by *Joyful Noise: Poems for Two Voices* by children's author Paul Fleischman, these poems, both playful and serious, can be written by students at all grade levels, and students definitely benefit from the opportunity to read a variety of these poems before they tackle their own. NCTE's ReadWriteThink site also offers valuable material designed to help students write two-voices poems, and, though the lesson "Moving toward Acceptance through Picture

Books and Two-Voice Texts" (Davenport and Irvin) is geared toward elementary school students, it includes samples as well as planning and drafting forms that may help high school students determine their topics and organize their ideas.

Sometimes two-voice poems spring spontaneously out of class discussion and can be a powerful tool for creating understanding and even compromise among students on opposing sides of an issue. Imagine two students who hold opposing political views creating this two-voice poem together: "I am a liberal / I am a conservative." Certainly, the two columns would present highly diverse views, but might these two students find themselves both speaking a line such as "I am an American," or "I am a patriot," or "I believe in freedom"? Just the act of having to compose a poem *together*—and together performing it for the class—offers the opportunity for cooperative effort and may provoke understanding about why each holds the view they do.

Despite the title, a two-voice poem can also be written by just one poet. In that case, the poet takes on the job of expressing two diverse viewpoints. This is an interesting exercise because it forces the writer to see both sides, even if they feel committed to one. A student who is against gun control, for example, might find, as they compose the opposing column of the poem, convincing reasons to support the other side, or perhaps they will discover beliefs that unite the two sides. This kind of activity asks students to stand in someone else's shoes to see the world from a different perspective, and that is a step toward tolerance. One point of caution here, however. It would be inappropriate and insensitive for students to be asked to write a poem from a perspective of which they have no genuine knowledge A student shouldn't attempt to speak in the voice of a student of a race or religion or sexual orientation that they know little about. Those dialogues should be left for two students who bring authentic experience to the work.

A workable variation on this asks students to use the two-voice design to contrast the views of characters in the literature they read. To do this, students rely on material in the text to create two different voices expressing different views, and in doing so they adopt an identity different from their own. In this activity, a student steps out of their own life to take on the persona of a fictional character. An example of this might be a two-voice poem between Lena Younger from *A Raisin in the Sun* and Amanda Wingfield from *The Glass Menagerie*. Both are strong women, deeply devoted to their children, but their love and commitment to their offspring shows itself in disparate ways and underlines how differently each approaches life because of their unique backgrounds and experiences. Writing such a poem challenges students to do a close reading of the text and to express their understanding of the text in a creative way. At the same time, students step out of their own lives to take on the experiences of someone quite different from themselves. If two students collaborate on such a poem, they engage in serious one-on-one conversation, and their poem can create a strong impetus for more classroom conversation when they perform their work aloud.

And a Few Other Thoughts

A few things I've learned through years of classroom experience don't fit into a category but do make difficult conversations easier and more productive.

As in most aspects of life, humor can be a lifesaver. A little laughter in the midst of an impassioned argument can make all the difference and allow opposing parties to bond a bit through shared laughter and to then move forward with the discussion in a respectful way. This is not to say that a teacher or student should ever make light of the serious topics that engender these sorts of discussion, but a well-placed and appropriate humorous comment can actually help a discussion. If we can laugh together, we can likely go on in a positive manner. Consider this: "Laughter not only gives conversation rhythm, but also regulates intimacy, releasing tension, communicating emotion, performing a similar job to those dials you twiddle on stereos, equalizers. Without its pulse, talk feels dead and social syntax buckles, because in very precise ways, laughter synchronizes conversation's dance" (Blyth 147–48). Or as Mark Twain said in his *Mysterious Stranger Manuscripts*, "Against the assault of laughter, nothing can stand," even, I would say, adolescent anger.

This next point is an important word of caution. Teachers should never expect a student to speak for their group, be it based on racial, religious, sexual, or any other form of identity. As I've noted, the school in which I teach is composed of students who are predominantly white. Students of color are in the minority in most of my classrooms. It can be easy to think it reasonable to defer to the opinions of an African American student, for example, when issues relating to Black culture and experience are part of the conversation. The truth is, however, this is both insensitive and dangerous. Not only does it put that one student unfairly on the spot, but it conveys the message to other students that all African Americans think alike. It's never a student's responsibility to be the spokesperson for any racial, ethnic, religious, or gender group, and though we can all learn from those whose experience, particularly in terms of identity, differs from our own, the sharing of such experiences needs to be entirely voluntary.

There are times when individual students will, on their own, speak up and offer a window into their own experience that may differ greatly from that of most of the students, and this absolutely helps their peers see from a new perspective. Jenny did that when she spoke about what it means for her to have Asperger's. Another one of my students often talked about her biracial heritage, and her openness allowed her classmates to ask questions and develop a better understanding of racial identity. One sophomore boy, a practicing Buddhist, never mentioned his religious beliefs until, as a class, we read Hermann Hesse's *Siddhartha,* and then he was eager to share his knowledge and experience with the class. I welcome these moments when students bring themselves and their unique experiences to our classroom conversations, and they know there is always an open invitation—but no pressure—for them to do so.

And finally, I believe that difficult conversations demand that teachers acknowledge the difficulty—and their own humanity. We need to admit to students the trepidation we all feel when we approach "dangerous" topics. I tell students about that censor in my head who had a much easier job twenty years ago, and I also describe uncomfortable moments of conversation when I've found myself in direct opposition to colleagues and friends in terms of political views. I believe that it's perfectly all right for teachers to express their own discomfort should a topic provoke such a feeling and that this sort of admission can help students as they grapple with sensitive issues. We teachers also need to be honest with ourselves and, if appropriate, with our students when personal experience colors our reactions. That's human, and we need to help students understand that. Students need the example of teachers who model how to admit and process emotion and yet not let it interfere with the intellectual exchange of ideas.

Resources for Teachers

There is a wealth of excellent information available to guide teachers as we facilitate difficult conversation in our classrooms. While this material may be especially helpful to new teachers, all teachers can benefit from reviewing the ideas and techniques the organizations described in this section offer.

For high school classrooms, two of the best and most well-known resources are Learning for Justice (www.learningforjustice.org) and Facing History and Ourselves (www.facinghistory.org). Each is geared to school classrooms and each offers an extensive collection of teaching ideas and materials.

Established in 1991 as Teaching Tolerance and renamed in 2021, "Learning for Justice seeks to uphold the mission of the Southern Poverty Law Center: to be a catalyst for racial justice in the South and beyond, working in partnership with communities to dismantle white supremacy, strengthen intersectional movements and advance the human rights of all people" (Learning for Justice).

What I especially appreciate about this organization is that it directly addresses the idea of antibias in a wide variety of spheres, including race, gender, religion, and ability, and offers an equally wide array of teaching resources on all these topics. Even a quick search of "How to facilitate difficult conversations" elicits numerous articles and activities with reading material, concrete suggestions, and advice for teachers.

Learning for Justice also offers two excellent publications (both available as a PDF), the first "Civil Discourse in the Classroom: Tools for Teaching Argumentation and Discussion" (Shuster) and the second *Let's Talk: A Guide to Facilitating Critical Conversations with Students* (Learning for Justice). These multipage booklets address such topics as argument literacy, ground rules for discussion, and the creation of a discussion-friendly classroom, and include specific activities for students and the teacher. Teachers eager to encourage classroom conversation on controversial topics—or those who are apprehensive about doing so—will find these publications an invaluable resource.

As the Facing History and Ourselves website explains, "Through rigorous historical analysis combined with the study of human behavior, Facing History's approach heightens students' understanding of racism, religious intolerance, and prejudice; increases students' ability to relate history to their own lives; and promotes greater understanding of their roles and responsibilities in a democracy" ("Why Facing History"). To this end, the organization offers a vast selection of materials for teachers, including lesson plans, readings, teaching strategies, videos, artwork and more. Teachers can also access professional development opportunities such as webinars and online courses as well as videos. Specific aspects of the site address the topic of hard conversations, including the PDF resource "Fostering Civil Discourse: How Do We Talk about Issues That Matter?" and the webinar "Navigating Difficult Conversations: Building Trust," with a list of classroom activities and other resources that teachers can implement in their classrooms. Also included on this topic are numerous articles and lesson plans, complete with essential questions, learning objectives, and activities that prepare students to tackle difficult discussions.

While I would first direct teachers to these two sites because of their materials designed expressly for high school classrooms, I'm including here some other websites that also offer teachers valuable material to help them guide difficult conversations in the classroom. I think it's worth noting that three of these websites are connected to colleges and universities, where not only are difficult conversations welcomed and encouraged but where educators receive intensive training on how to facilitate these conversations. It's telling to note that my first Google search of "difficult conversations in high school classrooms" produced an article on difficult conversations between teacher and parent and teacher and colleagues. That was followed by a series of entries focused on difficult conversations in college and university settings. I had to scroll down to the bottom of the page before I found anything geared primarily toward high school teachers. The next page of the search offered not much more.

If I wanted to put a positive spin on this, I'd say that the material offered by institutions of higher learning informs secondary school teachers as well—and, if you know what you're looking for, it does. But something tells me this is not its intent. This material is meant to help those who educate college-age students promote meaningful and intense classroom dialogues that will ultimately produce intelligent, informed, and civil citizens, and, moreover, most of this website material is an accompaniment to training for faculty. These resources consistently note the problems inherent in encouraging difficult conversations, and the reasons why we must continue to encourage them. They offer specific, detailed recommendations and suggestions as well as theoretical underpinnings to support the need for serious classroom conversation about controversial issues. I would highly recommend that teachers spend time looking at these sites. I would also suggest that high school teachers begin to question why the pursuit of difficult conversations is mainly the province of higher learning, particularly since we know very well that many of our students will never enter a college or university. If students are to explore with one another the issues that are so important to their own personal development as well as to the continued development of our democracy and the good of the world as a whole, they need to do so in our classrooms.

Faculty in institutions of higher learning also benefit from extended training in the facilitation of difficult conversations. Perhaps some of us in secondary schools have been lucky enough to have a day of professional development or a workshop offering or two to help guide us. But that is not enough, and the lack of training made available to high school teachers says that those in power either don't see the purpose of difficult classroom conversations—or they fear the possibility of them. Either way, if left on our own, it's imperative that we make the effort to educate ourselves.

Some of the best resources I have found are listed below. There are numerous excellent websites connected to colleges and universities across the country, but three here offer specific, user-friendly material that is relevant to the difficult conversations we might hold in our high school classrooms. The fourth website includes a "community of resources" that extends to facilitating difficult conversations across our society. Though all of the websites I've investigated offer some similar material, suggestions for specific teaching strategies and techniques differ from site to site. Also, every site includes lists of further resources, and a teacher can get happily lost in the material. This, I think, is a good thing, and I feel confident that whatever concerns teachers have about encouraging and facilitating difficult conversations will be addressed through some exploration.

> The University of Alaska Anchorage (UAA) is what I consider a "go to" site (www.uaa.alaska.edu/academics/institutional-effectiveness/departments/center-for-advancing-faculty-excellence/difficult-dialogues/handbooks/start-talking/). It presents an exceptional collection of teaching material found in "Start Talking: A Handbook for Engaging Difficult Dialogues in Higher Education" (Landis), a 2008 publication sponsored by the Ford Foundation's Difficult Dialogues initiative ("Difficult Dialogues"). The 256-page handbook (available as a PDF) includes strategies and activities to help teachers address critical social issues and controversial topics and includes faculty input on these activities.
>
> The Center for Teaching at Vanderbilt University (https://cft.vanderbilt.edu/guides-sub-pages/difficult-dialogues/) presents an excellent array of resources, including excerpts from the above mentioned UAA publication "Start Talking." The website also includes detailed, specific teaching strategies, podcasts, and a helpful list of additional resources to foster difficult conversations.
>
> The University of Florida offers its own more abbreviated "Handbook for Facilitating Difficult Conversations in the Classroom" (Vogelsang and McGee), also in a PDF version (teach.ufl.edu/wp-content/uploads/2016/07/Handbook-for-Facilitating-Difficult-Conversations2.pdf). Written by teachers for teachers, the handbook includes a variety of techniques and approaches for creating classrooms that welcome hard conversations. The website includes extensive lists of additional resources and links to help produce effective discussion.
>
> The Listen First Coalition (www.listenfirstproject.org) is "a community of 400+ organizations (the bridging field) bringing Americans together across differences to listen, understand each other, and discover common interests" ("Listen First Project"). The coalition sponsors a National Week of Conversation each April and, through its various partners, including America Talks (https://americatalks.us), offers articles, materials, and opportunities designed to help Americans connect to one another across the wide divides that separate us. From conversation tips to

bridge-building skills to face-to-face conversation activities, this group and its individual partners provide resources that help all Americans learn from one another and relate to each other with respect.

There is one more resource I'd like to offer, one that all we need to do is put in front of students for it to have an effect on them. This is a TEDx talk, delivered in 2019 by then high school student Sadhika Prabhu. "Courageous Conversations" is a seven-and-a-half-minute video that tackles the issue of injustice and inequality by encouraging what Prabhu calls "courageous conversations" (www.youtube.com/watch?v=fizDm4v8B0Q). These are conversations in which those in opposition share their beliefs and fully listen to one another. Her words are heartfelt and intelligent and will definitely resonate with high school students.

While it's true that difficult conversations are difficult, they are not impossible—and they are necessary. For teachers and students alike, these kinds of conversations demand interest, openness, backbone, and, on a very practical level, preparation. As teachers we cannot simply plunge our students into emotionally charged conversations and expect anything positive to come of it. As with any challenging task, participants need to develop specific essential skills if they are to find success. But they also must be willing to approach such conversations with an open heart, and with what Emily Chamlee-Wright of the Institute for Humane Studies calls "good faith." This term resonates with me, and I believe with students. When speaking at Beloit College, Chamlee-Wright was asked by a sophomore, "'What can we do to keep the conversation positive?'" Her response: "'We could all do a better job of assuming good faith,'" and she later reflects on what that phrase means:

> Assuming good faith means that we expect our conversation partner is interested in learning from us and is seeking to understand our point of view. It means that we should assume, unless we have good evidence to the contrary, that their intent is not to deceive or to offend. We can certainly point out when an error has been made or why offense has been taken, but it should be with the intent of making the conversation better, not closing it down. (Chamlee-Wright)

We are asking much of our students when we ask them to practice this kind of good faith, and I don't believe we can do so unless we as adults model it in all our interactions. We know young people have learned the language of bluster and bullying from too many of those in the spotlight of our society. We need to offer them another example, the kind of example that will keep conversations moving in classrooms where students can develop the competencies necessary to address the complex issues so prevalent in our world—and that will ultimately give students the courage to confront difficult issues with the words, "Can we talk?"

7

Where Speaking and Writing Intersect

Good writing is good conversation, only more so.

—Ernest Hemingway

A few years ago, I wrote a book called *Speak for Yourself: Writing with Voice.* I was motivated to write that book because it seemed that, in recent years, my students' writing had deteriorated. It wasn't that they lacked the basic skills, and they certainly were well versed in the standards, having spent all of their academic years preparing for standardized tests, but their writing was flat and, frankly, boring because it was devoid of voice. I felt that if I could give my students both the impetus and the license to write as they spoke, their writing would come alive and be a true expression of their selves. I still believe that, and I shape my teaching of writing around that philosophy.

So in the classroom I continue to design assignments that emphasize the importance of voice, and I consider voice a priority when I assess a final paper. When we study literature, we always talk about the writer's unique voice, and we try to figure out exactly what it is that makes Lorrie Moore different from Lydia Davis, or John Steinbeck different from J. D. Salinger. But what I've come to realize is that part of the reason my students struggle with voice on paper is that they aren't comfortable with their own speaking voice. For them, human interaction is most commonly carried out on a screen via a text, an Instagram post, or an emoji. Sherry Turkle writes of a college senior who tells her, "Anything having to do with the voice feels like an interruption" (45). Conversation, what those of older generations see as a natural means of human connection, is for young people an awkward and uncomfortable undertaking, something to be avoided. Teenagers have long been accused of being uncommunicative, especially in the presence of adults, but this recent inability to talk to others extends further, and young people are well aware of this. Their reflections indicate their understanding of their limited capacity to talk to one another:

> I feel that people don't talk much.... I feel that we have mastered the art of small talk, yet rarely do we have meaningful conversations.... A lot of the conversations I have are simple and short, but maybe something is wrong with the way I talk to most people.

> I personally struggle with conversation in class and sometimes outside. When there's a conversation going on in class I feel obligated to speak but have trouble coming up with things to say on the spot. And that can go for any conversation too, whether it's coming up with a new point or subject, or it's just coming up with a response.... I think conversations can be useful sometimes, but other times I'm too busy trying to come up with something to add to focus 100% on what's being said by others. I like to have time to prepare for conversation and come up with well-worded points before I speak out loud.

> Everyone has gotten so used to talking over texts that nowadays kids have no face to face social skills. People can't even look people in the eye anymore when meeting and shaking hands.

And though the following writer might agree with his peers, he doesn't seem to see conversation as an issue:

> I think that conversation is highly overrated in life. My parents are always telling me to improve my social skills and talk to new people. I think that social skills aren't needed in life, as asking a person, "Which way is the library?" or "Can I have a salad and breadsticks, please?" does not require skill. You don't necessarily need "skills" to talk to others.

Is it any wonder that so many students struggle with voice? If conversation is defined as ordering in a fast-food restaurant, if it's simply small talk, if it needs to be rehearsed, and if we've lost the ability to look each other in the eye when we talk, then is there any reason to assume that adolescents *have* an authentic voice—or one they want to share? I read comments such as these and feel disheartened, wondering if we have gone past the point where young people can even develop a real voice.

But one thing that encourages me is this: how interesting it is to see the difference in writing styles between those students who do, according to their own admission, enjoy conversation compared to those who do not. Look, for example, at these two pieces, both written by high school seniors of the same academic level. The first piece is the student's entire freewrite; the second is a bit less than half of the second student's freewrite.

Example #1

I think people talk and have conversations when the topic is appealing to them and they feel strongly about it. Another way is when they're in a comfortable environment and like the people they are talking with. Phones have made people more shy and less able to talk face to face.

Example #2

I mean, like honestly? I love talking and I feel like I literally never shut up. Especially in the classroom. I feel like sometimes classroom conversations aren't fun or engaging because most people could care less about what we're discussing. This is incredibly true when we have to talk about characters we don't like, in a plot that bores us, set in a time period no one relates to. Our generation's culture is based on "relatability." If something or someone does not have a resemblance or relatable factor to us, we lose interest, and by extension, the conversation is gone. Words are spoken to get a participation grade, but not because we genuinely care about what's being said. However, when discussions get to topics people can relate to and they feel comfortable /safe admitting that, that is when people actually get talking in earnest.

I don't think anyone would disagree that the second is the more engaging example. Though the opening two lines could have been written by Holden Caulfield, I feel pretty confident I could identify the actual author, although these freewrites were anonymous. This is because the second piece has voice and that writer's voice so vividly echoes the voice with which she speaks in class. The writer communicates personality and passion, and so the writing has power and is convincing. Though both writers are essentially saying the same thing, the author of the first example simply states an opinion. The author (and I have *no* idea who this writer is) may have *felt* strongly about the issue, but the writing doesn't indicate that, nor does it indicate any real desire to make the reader understand the writer's position. If I were to guess, I'd say this first example was written by a student who rarely spoke in class and the second by a far more loquacious classmate—and obviously one who freely admits to that.

What we see in these two pieces is a demonstration of the connection between the speaker's voice and the writer's voice. This is not to say that one cannot exist without the other or that there can't be some distinct differences between the two, and certainly many writers are notorious for introversion and a desire to stay somewhat hidden behind their written words. As teachers, however, our job is to nurture students' development in both areas—written and oral expression—as we help them develop the skills and strengths needed to have a voice in the world. To do so, we need to offer our students writing challenges that encourage voice and, in the process, improve their ability to speak. I see these challenges and activities as permeating the entire writing process.

To illustrate this and to show how voice on paper and voice in practice connect, I'm offering here one specific writing assignment. The process through which students complete this assignment, however, is definitely adaptable to virtually any topic or subject.

It's Not Fair!

I doubt there are many teenagers who have not at one time or another declared, "It's not fair!" The details of the situation will vary; it may not be fair that you can't stay out until midnight, get a new iPhone, or play the lead in the school play. On a more serious level, it may not be fair that your mother has cancer, that you've been the victim of a racist slur, or that college is out of your financial reach.

When my students begin this assignment—a personal narrative that captures an experience that to the writer felt unfair—they first participate in various brainstorming activities, including listing, drawing, freewriting, and the like, aimed to help them determine what it is they really want to write about. Once they come up with the experience they think they want to write about, they then orally *tell* their story to someone else in the class.

This is a great way to get students to recollect in detail the experience they want to relate—and it's a wonderfully sneaky way to incorporate conversation into the classroom. If I were to say to my students, "Pick a partner and together talk about unfairness in your lives and your reaction to it," I suspect my words would be met with a loud silence. That topic is too broad; that directive too intimidating. But if I ask students to tell a partner of their choice a story of one personal experience that felt unfair, most begin talking readily. I encourage the speaker to talk from the heart and to tell the story honestly and in detail. I encourage the listeners to ask questions, to add their own observations, and to feel free to express their emotional reaction to the story. In short, without ever saying so, I encourage the pair to have a conversation, "an unrehearsed intellectual adventure" (Armstrong). If I hear a pair go briefly in an unexpected direction—say, for example, that the story of not making the soccer team because the coach didn't like you becomes a conversation about why soccer is superior to football—I'm happy, because it means they are truly conversing, sharing and connecting. It's possible that this offshoot conversation might peripherally benefit the written piece, but it's certain that this unscripted sharing of ideas will allow these students to experience the pleasure of conversation and, I hope, crave more.

When the storytelling and the one-on-one conversation it provokes have ended, I generally reconvene the entire class for a wider discussion. Since all of the students have been involved in thinking about the idea of unfairness and about specific instances when they have experienced it, I can safely assume they all should have something to say. Whether they will say it, however, is another issue. But the point is, this conversation is inclusive; everyone has had time to think and process and talk about what they perceive to be unfair and how unfairness has impacted their lives. As we all know from our own personal experience, some conversations feel exclusive. We've all sat on the sidelines when people are talking about something we know nothing about. As adults we hope we might learn something as we sit there silently. As adolescents we may simply feel self-conscious. But by using a process such as this, a one-on-one sharing of a personal story that may have wider ramifications in the world, all students are welcomed into the larger conversation. and with luck this gets everyone thinking and talking.

"So," I say, "who has a story they want to share? Or—" (and this is the question I frankly prefer as it generally opens the door for more students) "who *heard* a story they wish their partner would share?"

A few hands pop up. I nod to a girl near the windows.

"Morgan's got a great story," her partner, Hannah, says earnestly.

Morgan's cheeks redden and she looks down. Morgan doesn't participate often, and I wonder where this will go. Other hands are still in the air, but I decide to ignore them for a minute.

"Morgan," I say encouragingly, "do you want to tell your story?"

She looks at Hannah and seems to be deciding. Hannah cheers her on. "It's about discrimination against girls."

That catches everyone's attention. Hands go down and everyone is looking at Morgan—which may or may not be a good thing. She may fold completely or else—

"Okay, well," Morgan takes a deep breath. "I applied for this job at a landscaper where my brother works. And I know just as much about landscaping as he does," she says emphatically, as if the entire class is about to dispute her. "So the boss, this guy in his fifties, I think, kept calling me 'sweetheart' and telling me this wasn't a job for a girl."

There's a unified murmur of outrage from students in the class, male and female alike, and that inspires Morgan to continue with a fiery story of what she sees as blatant discrimination.

"You could sue him, I think," a student says as, moments later, Morgan wraps up the tale, ending with the despondent admission that she's still looking for a part-time job.

I'm not surprised that I don't have to do a thing to keep this conversation going. Morgan's story has opened up a wellspring of fury, particularly from female students who have been told too often that their gender limits their abilities. But while these young women are eager to tell their own stories, there is more to the conversation. Students begin to talk about gender differences and gender stereotypes. In a brief span of thirty minutes or so, they talk about military service, childbearing, unequal pay, and self-defense. This is not a well-organized conversation—but then is any genuine conversation ever truly organized? It's true that as adults who enjoy participating in conversation we learn how to ask pertinent questions, make relevant connections, and smoothly segue from one topic to another. My students don't know how to do that—yet. They haven't had enough practice talking to one another about things that matter and things that rouse them to speak. These finer conversational skills elude them, but I know that if I offer enough opportunities for them to talk, along with some guidance in the art of conversation, they will develop these skills. But what this boisterous and unwieldy conversation has proved to me is that they possess those two qualities so necessary for any meaningful conversation—attention and interest (Blyth 14). And as students now begin their written pieces, they have, through time spent talking, explored more fully the idea of unfairness. Some, at this stage, even make the decision to write a different story, one that stirs in them the kind of passion that Morgan's tale has stirred in all of us.

At this point, the time has come to write the first draft. I usually give students two or three days to do so, reminding them to think about how they told their story to their classmate. When students tell a story to a peer, they almost always tell it in an authentic voice. It may be rambling and repetitious, it may be full of slang and sloppy grammar, and emotion may override explanation, but the voice is real, and often it's voice that draws us into a story. I also tell them to recall the questions their classmate asked and the parts of the story that seemed to provoke the most interest. I continue to emphasize the importance of writing the story in a voice that is as genuine as the one they spoke in. This is an enormous challenge for many students because, throughout their years of education, they have been taught a strange sort of voice I call "school speak." It's a voice that inevitably feels distant and dull and artificial, but it's a voice that earns high scores on standardized tests and has come to be viewed as a model of "good writing." It's a voice that follows every rule of grammar, one that would never begin a sentence with "And" or use a contraction. It's a voice that fits inside a template. It's a voice that ultimately renders the writer indistinguishable from their peers.

One of the simplest and best ways for students to discover on their own the authenticity of the voice they use in their writing is for them to read their work aloud. That is one important reason why I'm adamant that my students read their own drafts out loud when they are sharing their writing in response groups rather than simply pass the papers around the group. If a writer stumbles over their own written words, then it's likely that those words are not natural to the content and cadence of their speaking voice, and instead constitute the voice—or lack of voice—of "school-y" writing; it's stilted, stunted language that lacks individuality or identity.

Throughout the writing process that shapes this assignment, students are moving between their speaking voice and their writing voice, and strengthening both. The conversations they have in response groups allow them to improve not only their words on the page but also their ability to communicate with others. As one student writes in a reflection, "I think conversation helps form relationships. It teaches you how to tolerate criticism and to understand different people's lives and opinions." I believe these comments were meant in a more general sense and aren't just about conversation within response groups, but it's within these groups that some students begin to experience truly focused and meaningful conversation. The students meet often and don't change groups, so students build relationships through the conversations they share.

They also learn to appreciate differences not only in opinions and views but also in voice. As they work together through a writing assignment, they meet multiple times as writers continue to revise their work and seek feedback. Usually well before the end of the first term, most of them have abandoned school-speak writing and can recognize how different from one another each of them sounds on paper and how essential a unique voice is to the power of the writing. We talk about how often a writer's writing voice vividly reflects their speaking voice, and we discuss how those who speak in a sort of minimalist way, with straightforward, clipped sentences and minimal explication, generally write the same way, whereas those who are more verbose talkers tend to incorporate detail and description and sometimes meander away from the topic. This sort of writing instruction goes much deeper than a study of the supposed "rules" of good writing, and it isn't something for which the teacher can simply plan a week's worth of lessons and consider it done. Teaching—or maybe allowing—students to write with voice is something of a philosophical approach to the teaching of writing, one based on the belief that writing, like conversation, is an art and that our role as teachers is to give students the time, space, and encouragement to practice that art in a community of artists like themselves.

I know there are those who might contend that certain types of writing, such as personal essays, short stories, or opinion pieces, should reflect the writer's voice but would argue that analytical writing demands a more formal voice than that with which a student typically speaks. There is certainly a different expectation in terms of the style of any analytical writing, but the best of it, whether written by published authors or students, still shows a spark of the writer's personality, and the rhythm and flow of the writing is most effective when it's aligned with the way the writer speaks. Analytical writing is challenging for students for many reasons, but it becomes particularly difficult when students feel distant and detached from the writing, which is likely to happen when they are forced to adopt a voice that isn't their own. As we all know, a sense of ownership of the work is central to good writing, which is one reason why template-based writing so often falls flat and fails to engage the reader. So even when my students are writing a literary analysis or a research paper, I absolutely want to hear their voice in the work, and I encourage them to develop it by using the process described above. When you tell your ideas and talk out your points to those with whom you feel comfortable, you speak in a voice that is both honest and unaffected, and that can translate to the written word. My hope is that by nurturing each student's individual voice, I can get every student to realize that the best, the truest, and the most engaging communication, whether on paper or aloud, features that voice.

Clearly, students need varied opportunities to experiment with voice, and while sharing and storytelling in all its forms is an excellent activity, there are other low-risk assignments that help students understand the concept of voice and practice it. I always look for activities that combine both an oral and a written component. I like to use monologues and dialogues, those we find in the literature we read as well as ones we invent, as this literary form allows students to experience different voices and patterns of conversation. As they closely read and study such pieces, they begin to think about how conversation moves—and why it matters.

Susan Minot's "Green Glass," originally published in *The Atlantic* in 1992 and included in her recent collection, *Why I Don't Write: And Other Stories* (2020), is an excellent example of realistic—and revealing—dialogue. The story, told almost entirely in dialogue, captures the feelings, both expressed and repressed, of a twenty-something couple, Tom and Fran, as they navigate the conflicted emotions that a friend's wedding triggers in them. My students really like this story. Offering one of their highest points of praise, they tell me they find it "relatable," as the two characters attempt to deal with the predictable jealousies that arise when exes are in the picture. What we as readers know of these characters comes through their conversation, all that is both said and unsaid. I like to have students read the story aloud with one speaking Fran's words, another Tom's, and a third reading the remaining narration. Often they are interrupted in their reading by a student who can't help but say, "Ohh, I've said that exact same thing to my boyfriend," or by one who wonders, "Why do girls always say that?" Inevitably the story prompts conversation about relationships, and it's conversation that feels safe because, at least as it begins, it's about fictional characters. Generally, however, the conversation goes deeper, and students begin to talk about their own relationships, issues, and insecurities, and ultimately about the struggle to make themselves understood by the ones closest to them. This is natural conversation, and it's important conversation because it explores what it means to be human. It arises out of literature, but it becomes the stuff of real life, and students participate in it willingly.

At the same time that we are using this story to explore how conversation helps us make sense of ourselves as human beings, I can also draw on the story to help students understand the concept of voice. How does Fran sound different from Tom? What are the speech patterns and modes of expression that characterize each of them? How do word choice, pace, and the simple sound of the words work together to establish an individual voice for each character? How does the conversation convey emotion? And what about Minot's voice that supplies the bare bones of additional description? How would they describe that voice?

Activity with a story like this can go further. Students can role-play invented dialogues (either extemporaneous or written) that put characters in conflict, another perhaps involving Fran and Tom, or one with characters they have created. A parent and a child are popular choices, but sometimes students are far more creative. An insomniac wandering the streets at night might just meet an alien. Through the activity of role-playing, students grow more comfortable with face-to-face interaction. As with the Dr. Phil reenactment, it is, surprisingly, often the quieter students who volunteer to play a role, likely more confident when they can put themselves inside someone else's skin. The burden of being judged for one's words is lifted in this activity, so students speak with more self-assurance and take risks as they swap words back and forth. Sometimes, listening to the conversations they create, I find myself thinking it's silly that I'm taking time to allow high school students to *practice* the act of talking to one another, until I remind myself how infrequently many of them engage in anything longer than a brief verbal interaction, a quick question and answer, or a check-in. As is true with many skills, we often assume our students know more than they do, but in this case their comments, their reflections, and, perhaps most of all, their silences tell me that conversation is no longer a basic skill.

Teachers can take this role-playing activity to a more practical level as well by giving students the chance to participate in mock interviews and other more formal conversations. It's clear to me that they need this sort of practice to successfully communicate in the real world. In their reflections, my students plainly express the sheer panic they feel when talking to adults, especially those whom they feel a need to impress, and it seems this anxiety extends to their generation as whole:

> Just as playing the piano takes practice, so do social skills. iGen'ers are not practicing their in-person social skills as much as other generations did, so when it comes time for the "recital" of their social skills, they are more likely to make mistakes onstage when it matters: in college interviews, when making friends in high school, and when competing for a job. Life's social decisions are still made primarily in person, and iGen gets less experience with such situations. In the next decade we may see more young people who know just the right emoji for a situation—but not the right facial expression. (Twenge 91)

Most adolescents recognize that there is a difference between talking to a friend or family member versus talking to a college representative or a potential employer, and with that recognition comes the awareness of different voices that we use, depending on the situation. As one student (a self-proclaimed "very talkative person") writes, "I've noticed that people talk different when they are with different people. People talk differently to teachers than they would to classmates. . . . It's funny to see so many change their talking style." There seems to be a bit of disapproval for the variation here, but it's definitely true that we learn through life experience that we may need to present ourselves somewhat differently depending on the situation. Just as those students who seem to feel that a "Hey Ms. _________" is an acceptable salutation need some edification, so too do students need to understand that we each possess a range of different voices, particularly in terms of level of formality, and that different situations call for a choice of voice. This might be an opportunity to further discuss with students the slight shift in voice between that used in creative writing versus analytical writing. It's valuable for students to have the chance to experience a simulated job or college interview where they can experiment with language and actions (and maybe even try out that eye contact), potentially reducing their panic when they find themselves in such a real-life situation. As with the previous dialogue activity, students should act out these conversations to improve their communication skills, but they can also work on their written skills by writing out their dialogues, either in a play format or as part of a story narrative.

I'd also suggest here that when we're called on to write college recommendations, we should ask students to come *talk* with us. Most frequently, at least in my experience, students complete a form generally developed by the guidance office that asks them to list interests and abilities, awards and achievements, potential college plans, and so on, which we can use to augment our own portrayal of the particular student. Frankly, I find these forms fairly useless. I want to have a conversation with that student who trusts me to write them a recommendation. I want to know what really matters to that individual—and I can tell that when their face lights up and words pour out. I want the student to verbalize their hopes and plans, and I'm happy if they ask questions or seek my input. As much as I think I know each of my students in a classroom situation, I always discover something more, something often unique and special, when the two of us have a conversation. This is especially important for quieter students who rarely seek out such an opportunity. I think too that this time talking to me is something of a rehearsal for the student when there's an interview ahead, and it's also simply another opportunity for authentic conversation.

Connected to this college quest, I find it valuable for a student who wants me to offer feedback on their college essay to *first* talk to me about the topic of the essay, even if they've already written a draft of the piece. I think we all know that a major problem with college essays is that they can sound stilted and formulaic, and often one student's essay seems interchangeable with that of any other student. This is again because students have learned that "school writing" is good writing, despite clear evidence to the contrary. But when students *talk* about the subject of their essay, they generally speak with feeling, and, even without prompting, they incorporate the vivid and specific details that bring their stories and ideas to life. Meanwhile, I can ask questions and engage in a meaningful exchange about the topic. Once we've had this kind of conversation, I can send the student off to write or revise the essay, feeling fairly confident that the draft will be strong because it will have the voice—and I hope the passion—of its author.

Back in the classroom, another way to get students to explore the concept of voice in writing is to have them look at dramatic monologues. Sometimes I have students discuss the characteristics of the voice they hear in the monologue, and then I ask them to imagine and create the voice of the person who is listening. One powerful monologue is Langston Hughes's poem "Mother to Son." Written in the voice of an African American woman, this poem lets us hear her speak to her son, reminding him that life for her "has been no crystal stair." She admonishes him to work hard, to keep going, and to not give up, even though life is hard. In the poem, we hear nothing of the son's response, and so we can only imagine the other side of the conversation. I ask my students to think about how the son might react to his mother's words—and generally I can sense them putting themselves in his shoes. They consider where he might break in to interrupt, and they offer words he might say to get his ideas across. We can, through this activity, create a two-voice poem similar to that described in Chapter 6. I generally use this poem when I'm teaching Lorraine Hansberry's *A Raisin in the Sun*, and I sometimes ask students to imagine it is Walter, responding to his mother, and to speak and/or write his words This sort of activity allows students to look even more closely at individual voice while at the same time challenging them to demonstrate their understanding of specific characters we are studying.

In a similar way, I've used a poem by Katharyn Machan called "Hazel Tells Laverne," in which a working woman of a lower socioeconomic class describes to Laverne, presumably a fellow worker, a startling moment when, in the course of a day's work, a frog appears, promising her a better life in exchange for just one kiss. We hear only Hazel speak, but we can imagine an exchange between the two women and can create an entire conversation between them in words and on paper.

One thing to note is that both of these poems employ dialect to create a vivid portrayal of the character. Writing dialect is difficult, and even many published writers struggle to do it well. For me the study of dialect is important because it allows us to talk about qualities of speech particular to a specific region or group by examining the differences in grammar, pronunciation, word choice, and syntax. It is my hope that, by reading and discussing various dialects, students will develop a respect and appreciation for the blend of voices that is America. Students who have studied dialect in some depth may be up for the challenge of trying to write it, but others may be more comfortable writing the other side of the imagined conversation in a voice that is their own. The goal of these sorts of activities is to allow students the chance to practice conversation in a nonthreatening way. In the process, they are engaged in a close reading of the literature. In the case of these two poems, we read both a number of times, silently and aloud, looking for those places where a person might respond, as well as making certain that we understand what the speaker is really saying. Students also consider what we can ascertain based both on a person's spoken words and on the things that remain unsaid, which gives me a chance to talk about the importance of inference as well as the significance of silence. My goal with all of this is not to teach a unit on conversation that is separate from all the other work we do in an ELA class, but rather to make conversation—both as something we study and as something we *do*—an integral part of the classroom experience.

With that in mind, I'd also suggest that students might enjoy and benefit from simply writing dialogue. Somewhere around fourth grade, students seem to stop writing stories as class assignments. They are pushed on to more sophisticated forms of writing, such as the essay, the research paper, and, of course, the analysis. These forms don't offer students the opportunity to write dialogue among characters, so it's quite a challenge when, as high school students, they try to do so. Dialogue isn't easy to write, though before they attempt it, students often believe it is. Getting dialogue to flow and to sound natural is far more difficult than our favorite fiction writers would make us believe. For that reason alone, I like challenging students to create a character and to then write realistic dialogue for that character. This activity forces them to again consider the concept of voice in an effort to prevent their characters from all sounding alike.

The assignments my students like best are two that I have adapted from Anne Bernays and Pamela Painter, featured in *What If? Writing Exercises for Fiction Writers*. Assignment #37, "Dialogue Is All Art, Not Talk," challenges students to first discover how "real talk" is very different from the dialogue that writers craft. The writers note, "Dialogue has a difficult task in that it must simulate real talk at the same time it must artfully waste no words, reveal character, provide tension, and move the story forward" (104). As a class, we talk about characteristics of actual conversation, noting that speakers typically stumble and pause, repeat and reset, jump around, interrupt, and generally make a bit of a mess as they attempt to share words with one another. I then ask students to eavesdrop on a conversation that they overhear in their actual lives (being careful to caution them about not listening in on or repeating any truly personal material), and I ask them to try to transcribe such a conversation. When we share these "true life dialogues," students realize that this is not the stuff of a great story, and I read them more of Bernays and Painter's words: "Good dialogue is not at all the way human beings speak to each other—it's an approximation. Dialogue takes human speech and renders it condensed, highlighted, and pointed" (117). This realization allows us to have a serious conversation about the "ingredients" of actual conversation and to reflect on what participants need to bring to an authentic conversation.

Students then tackle Assignment #41, "A Verbal Dance: Not Quite a Fight," which challenges the writer to "write a dialogue between two people who know each other, each taking the opposite side of an issue" (Bernays and Painter 117). When I do this assignment in my Creative Writing class as part of a fiction unit, students have already created a fictional character, so they can pair up and easily begin to fashion an argument between their two creations. In that situation, they are familiar with the characters they have crafted, and they know how these characters would react in various circumstances. As a result, students really enjoy this opportunity to let their characters square off. When I do this assignment in classes where students haven't been closely studying fiction techniques, however, I give them time to first imagine a scenario in which two people might find themselves in conflict, and then I ask each student to imagine one of the characters involved and create a brief character sketch. This allows the writer to have a better sense of how this particular character would talk in order to ultimately capture a realistic voice. I like having students collaborate on this dialogue because, in the process of thinking and rethinking, writing and rewriting, they are better able to determine whether a character sounds real and unique and true. Together they can make sure that the characters have voice. Often too, through their development of the conflict the characters face, students can practice varying ways of expressing opposing views and discover how much conversational styles can affect a contentious conversation.

For those who are always looking for an opportunity to do mini-lessons on grammar, punctuation, capitalization, and such, I can also assure you that this activity provides that occasion. My students' efforts to correctly format their dialogues sometimes make me laugh (or groan) as they sprinkle quotation marks here and there, punctuate in and outside the quotes, create paragraphs wherever they choose, and generally make random stabs at editing. But the fact is that students rarely have reason to write dialogue, so this assignment gives them a chance to learn some new skills, or skills they may have forgotten since their earlier story-writing years, and what they learn helps them to be better readers of literature.

I want to emphasize that throughout all of the activities described in this chapter, students talk. They talk with a partner, they talk with me, and they talk with the whole group. They share ideas about writing, they share thoughts about human behavior, and they share pieces of themselves. I don't have to say, "Today we are going to talk," nor do I have to stand in front of the room and talk to them. What happens is authentic communication among people engaged in similar pursuits. It is true conversation, and it creates better speakers, better writers, better thinkers, and better human beings.

8

Tricks of the Trade

The single biggest problem in communication is the illusion that it has taken place.

—George Bernard Shaw

I chose this chapter's title with purpose—and with concern. Some of the ideas that follow at times strike me as techniques, but at other times as tricks. I am not a fan of tricks, of supposedly clever ways to generate the sound of student voices in the classroom, and I use that phrase purposely too. Just because we hear the blur of voices in the classroom doesn't mean that students are talking, or at least talking in the way this book promotes. Genuine conversation is organic. It rises out of a need to express oneself in words that are authentic and reflect one's individuality, and it happens naturally. As Catherine Blyth writes, "Conversation is something bigger: It is the spontaneous business of making connections, whether for work, friendship, or pure, fleeting pleasure" (4).

"The spontaneous business of making connections." I like that. I like especially the word *spontaneous*, and that is why I hesitate to fully endorse some of these classroom techniques. When we as teachers orchestrate the way we want our students to converse with one another, we alter the dynamics of conversation by creating something different, something more like "school talk." This is why I oppose the use of sentence starters and talk stems and suggest instead that we give students space and time to figure out how to express themselves without the use of artificial aids. As I note in Chapter 5, "Don't Put Words in My Mouth," discussion techniques can at times actually serve as a deterrent to authentic conversation. But at the same time, I recognize that every class—and every teacher—is different, and that there can be, for teachers and students alike, a benefit in having available some techniques that jump-start conversation. Many of those that follow are ones that teachers use frequently, which is another reason I back away from them. I've seen the word *Jigsaw* cause more than one student to roll their eyes and groan, "Again?" With that in mind, I'm also going to assume that teachers are well versed in Gallery Walks and Four Corners and Socratic seminars and don't need me to offer extensive explanations of each here. If you want descriptions of these activities, detailed material is easily available through a Google search. But if you use those techniques or any of the following judiciously, cautious of the frequency of use and willing to adapt the technique to fit a particular classroom style, then these ideas may be valuable in helping to stimulate classroom conversation. Most are not my invention, and most have been around so long that there's no clear agreement on the creator. Where appropriate I've added my own twists and cautions. The key thing teachers need to understand is that these activities don't in and of themselves equate with class conversation. They are instead ways of sparking ideas and stimulating minds to inspire that spontaneous conversation described above.

Write-Pair-Share—We are all, I'm sure, familiar with the Think-Pair-Share technique, and I've discussed my concerns about its limitations. But the Write-Pair-Share strategy asks students to each individually first write down their thoughts and ideas, thus ensuring that each *is* actually thinking about the topic before any sharing occurs. This has the added benefit of giving students a little more practice in low-stakes writing, and, as students are freewriting on the topic, you can circulate the room, offering help and encouragement to those who need it.

I Was Wondering . . .—This is a strategy similar to Rothstein and Santana's Question Formulation Technique, with a few changes. I've used this when planned discussion questions are met with utter silence. Maybe students have read the assigned pages of *Julius Caesar*, but there's nothing going on in class to prove that. To stir up conversation, I ask them to form small-group circles and tell them that, in a five-minute time frame, each group needs to come up with as many questions as it can as students, one by one around the circle, contribute questions. One person in the group writes down each question just as it was asked. Before they begin, I tell them that no one should answer a question. This activity works first and foremost to break the classroom silence and to get an energetic flow of ideas started. It even creates a friendly competition as each group vies to come up with the most questions. It also generates a wealth of questions that we as a class can then use to start a discussion, and it tells me what students found difficult in their reading and what needs to be discussed. And finally, and fortunately, rarely do they follow my admonishment to not answer questions. Inevitably, someone will respond to a classmate's question, and that gets real conversation started.

The Card Toss—As noted in Chapter 2, "What Research Tells Us," this activity, using a participation chip, is something of a last resort for me, but I have used it with a relative degree of success. When, even after repeated opportunities, students simply don't engage in class discussion, I greet each of them at the start of a period with three playing cards. As we begin a whole-class discussion with students seated in a circle, their goal is to get rid of their cards by contributing something worthwhile—be it a question or a comment—to the discussion. With their verbal contribution, they toss a card into the center of the circle. And just in case a student thinks they can get by saying something meaningless, I add this rule: Nonsensical comments result in a penalty of two additional cards.

The Talking Stick—Sometimes the opposite problem occurs in class, and all students want to talk. I had a colleague whom I highly respected who swore by the talking stick, and, though it's not something I've used often, I include it in her honor. Used by many Native American tribes, the talking stick gives whoever is holding it the floor to speak. Everyone else has to remain quiet and listening. When the speaker has concluded what they have to say, they hand the stick to another student, who can then speak or choose to pass it on to someone else. This technique is particularly effective in a class where many students want to speak and few want to listen. For some reason, the physicality of the stick itself has power.

The Talk Toss—This activity is somewhat similar to the talking stick—but somehow very different. It's definitely more playful than the talking stick, so it's better suited for lighter discussion and the quick exchange of ideas. It can often loosen up a class that seems reserved or timid or otherwise reluctant to share ideas, and it can get a number of students talking because it creates an easy atmosphere and little pressure. Using a light rubber ball (or, if you prefer even more frivolity, a beach ball), the teacher tosses the ball to one student, who then has to contribute something, generally something brief and pithy, to the discussion. That student then tosses the ball to another student, who adds comments and tosses it again. Somehow the mere act of catching the ball distracts from the pressure of speaking in class and encourages more students to speak.

Meets and Greets—I like to be sure that students don't get stuck in a rut of talking only to their closest friends or to those who sit closest to them in class. So, to alleviate the potential for this, I tell them they are going to get to know *all* the members of their class. I first give them a few minutes to come up with some key questions they might ask each other about the topic at hand. Then, armed with a notebook or clipboard and their questions, they get up and wander about the room, knowing they have twenty minutes to talk to a minimum of ten people. In these short, two-minute conversations, they need to ask a question or two about the topic and record the key points they heard, collecting material they can contribute to a whole-class discussion.

In a variation on this, I ask students to gather questions from at least ten of their peers on the topic we are going to discuss. When the whole class resumes, I ask students to put on the board the most interesting question that each collected, and this material becomes a stimulus for our class discussion.

Constructing a Conversation—This activity appears to students to be a writing activity but is in fact a discussion starter. Before students come into class, I post around the room, on separate pieces of construction paper, a series of questions, usually ten or so per class, related to the work we are studying. For example, having read Ann Beattie's "Sunshine and Shadow," students might find these kinds of questions: "*sunshine* and *shadow*. What do you think that means, both literally and symbolically?" "What do you think Beattie is saying about love in our culture?" "Beattie connects love and space travel and acid trips and bee-keeping suits in this story. What are the connections you see?" Students roam around the room and respond in writing to a certain number, usually seven or eight, of the questions on the construction paper. They can draw arrows and build on other students' responses (but no easy "I agrees" are allowed!), or they can offer their own new ideas. Often little groups hover around a question and spontaneous conversation begins. At the end of this written response, students form pairs or groups of three, and each group tackles one question, first reviewing and discussing the material on the paper and then formulating an "expert" response to contribute to the class conversation.

Get in Line—A quick way to gauge student opinion on an issue or idea is to ask students to form a line based on their level of agreement with a statement. So, for example, as a pre- or postreading activity with *The Glass Menagerie*, I ask students to read a series of statements related to the central ideas of the play. Such statements include: "It is selfish to leave your family behind to pursue your own dreams." "Staying safe is better than taking risks." "It is a parent's duty to see only the best in their child." For each statement, students designate a number from 1 to 10, 1 indicating total disagreement with the statement and 10 total agreement. Then I ask a student to pick a statement they want to discuss, and, once they make their choice, students form a line that wends its way around the room, based on their own level of agreement with the statement. Once they've formed a line, I tell students to talk to the people on both sides of them to share reasons for their placement—and to see if there are degrees of difference. Maybe, I tell them, you're not really an 8 but rather an 8 ½. I direct student to move accordingly as they discover these subtle differences, or if they change their opinions entirely. We repeat this process with a few statements on the original list, and then we reconvene as a class to have a full discussion.

This activity offers students an opportunity for one-on-one conversation and also allows them to rehearse their ideas and sometimes modify them before the whole class talks together. As a result, students are more confident about sharing their ideas with the larger group.

Conversation Circles—A very basic impetus to conversation among students is the use of a circular seating plan. The circle, with students able to look directly at one another, is infinitely more conducive to conversation than is a room of rigid rows where virtually all students are speaking to each other's backs and the only face they see is the teacher's. But more often than not, the class is too large and the room too small to form one big circle and so students have to sit in two semicircles. This, however, can work well for stimulating discussion. Students in the inner circle simply turn their desks so they are face to face with those in the outer circle. The teacher offers a question or topic for discussion, and each facing pair takes a brief time to talk to each other about it. The teacher then directs students in the inner circle to move one seat to the right and a new conversational duo is created. This process can continue for as long as the teacher feels is appropriate, and, at the conclusion, students have many thoughts and ideas to share with the entire class.

Building Blocks—Also known as Snowballing, this activity allows students to start a conversation on a small scale and then progressively expand the conversation to an increasingly larger group. Each student finds a partner and together they discuss an idea or topic until the teacher instructs each to find another pair, and then, in the group of four, they all share their ideas. The group of four next merges with another group of four, forming a group of eight, and the process continues until the entire class has joined in one large group. This activity especially benefits students who prefer small-group discussion and can gain confidence as the size of the group grows slowly. It also reminds students that they are all one community, even when we are separated into smaller groupings.

Again, I would remind us all that these activities don't on their own typically produce the kind of in-depth, intense, and inclusive conversation we want to achieve in our classrooms. They are, however, a helpful means of getting to that conversation because (1) they motivate our students to seriously think about the topic of discussion, (2) they build confidence by allowing for preliminary sharing of ideas on a small scale, and (3) they let students see that no one has the "answers" and that we are all engaged together in a search for them. And though I have called these strategies "tricks," the truth is there are no tricks when it comes to creating a classroom where students feel free to speak their minds—and equally free to change them. Instead, we need to rely on all we know about our students—and ourselves—to build a classroom community where students want to be heard and want to listen.

I want to offer one more effective resource, and one that is definitely *not* a trick. Celeste Headlee's 2016 TED Talk, "10 Ways to Have a Better Conversation," is highly entertaining, but it's also filled with wisdom and practical advice to help students as they learn to engage in good conversation. And yes, I'll admit that in eleven and a half minutes, she captures brilliantly what I have taken an entire book to try to say!

Conclusion

To be kind is more important than to be right. Many times, what people need is not a brilliant mind that speaks but a special heart that listens.

—F. Scott Fitzgerald

Not long ago, I received an email from a former student, now a junior in college. Eric is an exceptional young man. He is both mathematician and writer—and a bit of a philosopher. He is a person of intelligence and wit. He is deeply insightful and extremely kind. And he sometimes struggles with social interactions. In his email, Eric wrote, "Still, it does sadden me a bit at times at just how difficult it can be to find other people. I can sometimes feel a sort of overall feeling of isolation from society, as I sometimes feel almost completely unnoticed in a crowd of people as they pass by me on their phones."

My heart went out to Eric. But it was only as I responded with the words, "You're not alone in what you're feeling," that I realized how utterly true that is. In this twenty-first century, it is incredibly difficult for all of us "to find other people," and yet most of us keep trying.

In the course of writing this book, I've read many descriptions of conversation. But this one has stuck with me. In a 2016 essay, "Saving the Self in the Age of the Selfie," the historian James McWilliams says of real talk, "It demands that we introduce a fragile self into social space, throw the verbal dice, and hope for connection." I read those words and the risk feels palpable. And sadly, that risk has grown.

I write this conclusion as the pandemic eases, as we take off our masks, open our doors, and rejoin the world. We talk of a return to normalcy, which for many of us means the opportunity to reconnect with those around us. It seems as though it should be easy and joyful, and yet we're finding that it's inexplicably strange and awkward to be in the physical presence of those we have missed the most. Just as we bumble a bit as we reach out to hug or clasp hands, so too do we stumble as we open our mouths and start to speak. It's as if we've forgotten how to talk, as if we've become like the adolescents in our classrooms who find security in screens rather than in social encounters.

There are rational reasons for this discomfort. In an interview in *Vox*, Barnard College psychology professor Tara Well describes the difficulty we are having as we attempt social interactions beyond the Zoom screen:

> I think one of the things that happened during the pandemic is that we needed to modulate and adjust our level of intimacy, with face-to-face and being either seen way more than we were used to, or way less than we're used to.
>
> Conversations went that way, too.
>
> I think many of our conversations were either talking about personal trauma and life-changing events that were super, super heavy or wanting to divert ourselves into talking about TV shows and whatnot. How do you modulate between staying in reality and not denying everything that's happened? And also keep your sense of humor and be able to introduce new, interesting things to your conversations. (Abad-Santos)

In other words, how do you talk to another human being about things that matter? How do you look another person in the eye and open your heart? How do you connect?

I think that this slow return to normalcy has made me more fully understand something I only grasped intellectually before. I knew that my students struggled with conversation. I acknowledged that it was hard for them to give voice to their thoughts, and I sympathized with their struggle because I recognized that they were products of twenty-first-century technology with all its wonders—and frightening limitations. But where once, before that late winter of 2020, I sympathized with my students, now I empathize. Two years of physical distance and disruption, supposedly assuaged by that very same technology that both joins and distances us, have shown me that carrying on a face-to-face conversation can be a challenge, and I am still getting used to that. But I also know that those of us who are adults are lucky. We remember the pleasure of conversation. We'll sacrifice some temporary discomfort to experience once again the deep satisfaction true human connection brings. We will get our voices back. But for young people who have never really had the experience of connecting through conversation and who have now grown steadily more dependent on screens, the situation is different and far more dire. If there is ever a time that we need to promote meaningful conversation in our classrooms, it is now. As teachers we must offer ample opportunities for conversation, we must help our students find the courage to converse, and we must applaud them for their efforts. For all of us, reaching out is such a risk, and only the extraordinary reward—genuine human connection—makes that choice possible.

I began this book with a feeling of frustration. My students wouldn't, maybe couldn't, talk to one another, and I didn't know if I could help them. As I finish these pages, my frustration has been replaced with a sense of sadness. It's evident to me that many of my students have spent too many days of their lives lacking—and often longing for—the kind of connection that meaningful conversation brings. I can't change society, this internet age we all live in, but I have made a commitment to change the space we share, and I would hope every classroom teacher would make the same commitment.

The philosopher John Armstrong defines conversation as "civilized speech . . . more purposeful than chatter; more humane than gossip; more intimate than debate." Turn off the chatter, the gossip, and the debate, and what is left is something much deeper and much richer. If we can get our students to truly talk to one another, we can get them to fully engage in their learning. If we can get our students to speak their truth, we can give them a voice. If we can get our students to listen to each other, we can open their minds and instill in them the power of empathy. Finally, if we can do all of these things, perhaps we can get our students to acknowledge that this is what they have been missing and what they need. As Armstrong writes, "Secretly we yearn for real conversation, because we long to encounter the best and most substantial versions of other people. We long for the truth of ourselves to be grasped and liked by another person." Simply, it seems, we want to discover others and reveal ourselves and, in doing so, restore our humanity. I'm optimistic. I think it is possible for our students and for ourselves. I think we *can* talk.

Works Cited

Abad-Santos, Alex. "The Pandemic Has Made Small Talk Even More Painful." *Vox*, 1July 2021, www.vox.com/the-goods/22555596/pandemic-social-awkward-conversations.

"About StoryCorps." *StoryCorps*, 2020, storycorps.org/about.

"America Talks." 2022. https://americatalks.us.

Anderson, Monica, and Jingjing Jiang. "Teens, Social Media and Technology 2018." *Pew Research Center*, 31 May 2018, www.pewresearch.org/internet/2018/05/31/teens-social-media-technology-2018.

Armstrong, John. "The Art of Conversation." *The Conversation*, 21 June 2011, theconversation.com/the-art-of-conversation-1927.

Barnwell, Paul. "My Students Don't Know How to Have a Conversation." *The Atlantic*, 22 Apr. 2014, www.theatlantic.com/education/archive/2014/04/my-students-dont-know-how-to-have-a-conversation/360993/.

Bernays, Anne, and Pamela Painter. *What If? Writing Exercises for Fiction Writers*. Rev. & exp. ed., HarperCollins, 1995.

Blyth, Catherine. *The Art of Conversation: A Guided Tour of a Neglected Pleasure*. Gotham Books, 2009.

Brookfield, Stephen D., and Stephen Preskill. *Discussion as a Way of Teaching: Tools and Techniques for Democratic Classrooms*. 2nd ed., Jossey-Bass, 2005.

Burton-Hill, Clemency. "What Does a Conductor Actually Do?" *BBC Culture*, BBC, 31 Oct. 2014, www.bbc.com/culture/article/20141029-what-do-conductors-actually-do.

Carver, Raymond. "Fear." *All of Us: The Collected Poems*. Vintage Contemporaries, 2000, p. 60.

Chamlee-Wright, Emily. "The Presumption of Good Faith in Campus Conversation." *Inside High Ed*, 13 Aug, 2019, https://www.insidehighered.com/views/2019/08/13/need-presume-good-faith-campus-conversations-and-debates-opinion.

Cohen, Leah Hager. *I Don't Know: In Praise of Admitting Ignorance (Except When You Shouldn't)*. Riverhead Books, 2013.

Coleman, Peter. "Can't Touch This—Why Talking across Our Political Divide Is Not Enough." *The Hill*, 13 May 2020, thehill.com/opinion/campaign/497365-cant-touch-this-why-talking-across-our-political-divide-is-not-enough.

Cortese, Katie. "Firebug." *Carve Magazine, Honest Fiction*, 15 Dec. 2012, www.carvezine.com/story/2012-winter-cortese.

Davenport, April, and Karen Irvin. "Moving toward Acceptance through Picture Books and Two-Voice Texts." *ReadWriteThink.org*, National Council of Teachers of English, www.readwritethink.org/classroom-resources/lesson-plans/moving-toward-acceptance-through-1138.html.

"Difficult Dialogues." *Vanderbilt University*, Vanderbilt University, Mar. 2020, cft.vanderbilt.edu/guides-sub-pages/difficult-dialogues.

"Discover StoryCorps." *StoryCorps*, 2020, storycorps.org/discover.

Ellison, Ralph. "What These Children Are Like." *Teaching American History*, Sept. 1963, https://teachingamericanhistory.org/document/what-these-children-are-like.

Emerson, Ralph Waldo. "Self-Reliance." *Selections from Ralph Waldo Emerson: An Organic Anthology*, edited by Stephen E. Whicher, Houghton-Mifflin, 1976, pp. 147–68.

Faulkner, William. "A Rose for Emily." *The Norton Anthology of Short Fiction*, edited by Ronald V. Cassill, W. W. Norton, 1978, pp. 233–41.

Fleischman, Paul. *Joyful Noise: Poems for Two Voices*. Illustrated by Eric Beddows, Harper, 2019.

Frost, Robert. "Education." *Oxford Reference*, https://www.oxfordreference.com/view/10.1093/acref/9780191826719.001.0001/q-oro-ed4-00003970.

"Fulfilling the American Dream: Liberal Education and the Future of Work." Hart Research Associates, July 2018, aacu.org/research/fulfilling-the-american-dream-liberal-education-and-the-future-of-work.

Gewertz, Catherine. "Speaking Skills Top Employer Wish Lists. But Schools Don't Teach Them." *Education Week*, 25 Sept. 2018, www.edweek.org/ew/articles/2018/09/26/speaking-skills-top-employer-wish-lists-but.html?print=1.

Gordon, Emily Fox. "How I Learned to Talk." *The American Scholar*, 3 Sept. 2019, pp. 82–93, theamericanscholar.org/how-i-learned-to-talk/.

Hansberry, Lorraine. *A Raisin in the Sun*. Vintage Books, 1994.

Headlee, Celeste. "10 Ways to Have a Better Conversation." *TED*, April 2015, www.ted.com/talks/celeste_headlee_10_ways_to_have_a_better_conversation.

———. *We Need to Talk: How to Have Conversations That Matter*. Harper Wave, 2018.

Holmberg, Carrie, and Jamaal Muwwakkil. "Conversation in the Classroom." *Kappanonline.org*, Phi Delta Kappan, 27 Jan. 2020, kappanonline.org/ conversation-classroom-holmberg-muwwakkil.

Holzer, Madeleine Fuchs. "Teach This Poem: 'In This Place (An American Lyric)' by Amanda Gorman." *Poets.org*, Academy of American Poets, 20 Jan. 2019, poets.org/lesson-plan/teach-poem-place-american-lyric-amanda-gorman.

Hughes, Langston. "Mother to Son." *poetryfoundation.org*, Poetry Foundation, www.poetry foundation.org/poems/47559/mother-to-son.

Jiang, Jingjing. "How Teens and Parents Navigate Screen Time and Device Distractions." *Pew Research Center*, 22 Aug. 2018, www.pewresearch.org/internet/2018/08/22/how-teens-and-parents-navigate-screen-time-and-device-distractions.

Jost, Walter. "Lessons in the Conversation That We Are: Robert Frost's 'Death of the Hired Man.'" *College English*, vol. 58, no. 4, Apr. 1996, pp. 397–422, doi:10.2307/378852.

kaur, rupi. "Quotes." *Goodreads*, 2022, https://www.goodreads.com/author/quotes/807 5577.

Kirby, Dan, et al. *Inside Out: Strategies for Teaching Writing*. 3rd ed., Heinemann, 2004.

Landis, Kay, editor. "Start Talking: A Handbook for Engaging Difficult Dialogues in Higher Education." University of Alaska Anchorage and Alaska Pacific University, 2008, www.uaa.alaska.edu/Academics/Institutional-Effectiveness/Departments/Center-for-Advancing-Faculty-Excellence/Difficult-Dialogues/_documents/Start_Talking.Pdf.

Learning for Justice. "About Learning for Justice." The Southern Poverty Law Center, 2021, https://www.learningforjustice.org/about.

———. *Let's Talk: A Guide to Facilitating Critical Conversations with Students*. The Southern Poverty Law Center, 2019, https://www.learningforjustice.org/sites/default/files/2019-12/TT-Lets-Talk-December-2019.pdf.

Lempinen, Edward. "Want to Persuade an Opponent? Try Listening, Berkeley Scholar Says." *Berkeley News*, 26 June 2020, news.berkeley.edu/2020/06/26/want-to-per suade-an-opponent-try-listening-berkeley-scholar-says.

Lindbergh, Anne Morrow. "Argonauta" *Gift from the Sea*. Pantheon, 1955, pp. 89–110.

Lindblom, Ken, and Leila Christenbury. *Continuing the Journey 3: Becoming a Better Teacher of Language, Speaking, and Listening*. National Council of Teachers of English, 2019.

"Listen First Project." *listenfirstproject*.org, 2022, https://www.listenfirstproject.org.

Machan, Katharyn. "Hazel Tells Laverne." *Ithaca College*, ithaca.edu/faculty/machan/poetry.

McCarthy, Claire. "Anxiety in Teens Is Rising: What's Going On?" *healthychildren.org*, American Academy of Pediatrics, 20 Nov. 2019, www.healthychildren.org/English/health-issues/conditions/emotional-problems/Pages/Anxiety-Disorders.aspx.

McCarthy, John. "Extending the Silence." *Edutopia*, 10 Jan. 2018, https://www.edutopia.org/article/extending-silence.

McSpadden, Kevin. "You Now Have a Shorter Attention Span Than a Goldfish." *TIME*, 14 May 2015, time.com/3858309/attention-spans-goldfish.

McWilliams, James. "Saving the Self in the Age of the Selfie." *The American Scholar*, 29 Feb. 2016, theamericanscholar.org/saving-the-self-in-the-age-of-the-selfie.

Minot, Susan. "Green Glass." *Why I Don't Write: And Other Stories*. Random House, 2020, pp. 53–64.

Obama, Barack. "Obama to Graduates: Cultivate Empathy." *Northwestern University News*, 19 June 2006, www.northwestern.edu/newscenter/stories/2006/06/barack.html.

Peter D. Hart Research Associates, Inc. "Report of Findings." Association of American Colleges and Universities, 6 Jan. 2006, https://docplayer.net/8662639-The-association-of-american-colleges-and-universities-by-peter-d-hart-research-associates-inc.html.

Prabhu, Sadhika. "Courageous Conversations." TEDx Talks, *YouTube*, 6 June 2019, www.youtube.com/watch?v=fizDm4v8B0Q.

Resnick, Lauren B., et al. "Accountable Talk: Instructional Dialogue That Builds the Mind." *Educational Practices Series 29*, 2018, http://www.ibe.unesco.org/sites/default/files/resources/29_accountable_talk_instructional_dialogue_that_builds_the_mind.pdf.

Rideout, Victoria. "Social Media, Social Life: How Teens View Their Digital Lives." *Commonsensemedia.org*, 2012, https://www.commonsensemedia.org/sites/default/files/research/socialmediasociallife-final-061812.pdf.

Rotella, Carlo. "Silent Students Shortchange Themselves, and Others." *Boston Globe.com, Boston Globe*, 13 Sept. 2013, www.bostonglobe.com/opinion/2013/09/12/silent-students-shortchange-themselves-and-others/Ejtaro5N3cuICjDy61NG8K/story.html.

Rothstein, Dan, and Luz Santana. "The Right Questions." *ASCD*, 1 Oct. 2014, www.ascd.org/publications/educational-leadership/oct14/vol72/num02/The-Right-Questions.aspx.

Rubenstein, Susanne. "Chasing the Dream: Researching the Meaning of the American Dream." *Readwritethink.org*, National Council of Teachers of English, 2022, www.readwritethink.org/classroom-resources/lesson-plans/chasing-dream-researching-meaning-30925.html.

Shuster, Kate. "Civil Discourse in the Classroom: Tools for Teaching Argumentation and Discussion." *Learning for Justice*, Southern Poverty Law Center, 2010, https://www.learningforjustice.org/sites/default/files/2017-10/Civil-Discourse-v2-CoverRedesign-Oct2017.pdf.

"Social Media, Social Life: Teens Reveal Their Experiences, 2018." *Common Sense Media*, 10 Sept. 2018, https://www.commonsensemedia.org/research/social-media-social-life-teens-reveal-their-experiences-2018.

"Speaking of Psychology: The Decline of Empathy and the Rise of Narcissism." *American Psychological Association*, Dec. 2019, www.apa.org/research/action/speaking-of-psychology/empathy-narcissism.

Stahl, Robert J. "Using 'Think-Time' and 'Wait-Time' Skillfully in the Classroom." ERIC Digest (ED370885), May 1994, https://files.eric.ed.gov/fulltext/ED370885.pdf.

Steinmetz, Katy. "Teens Are Over Face-to-Face Communication, Study Says." *TIME*, 10 Sept. 2018, time.com/5390435/teen-social-media-usage.

Szymborska, Wisława. "Wisława Szymborksa—Poetry." *NobelPrize.org*, Nobel Prize Outreach AB 2022, 18 June 2022, https://www.nobelprize.org/prizes/literature/1996/szymborska/poetry/.

Tsai, Diana. "Can Conversations Add 15 Years to Your Life? The Science Says Yes." *Forbes* 31 July 2020, https://www.forbes.com/sites/dianatsai/2020/07/31/can-conversations-add-15-years-to-your-life-the-science-says-yes/?sh=56376cd139d2.

Turk, Gary. "Look Up." *Gary Turk*, 2016, garyturk.com/.

Turkle, Sherry. *Reclaiming Conversation: The Power of Talk in a Digital Age*. Penguin, 2016.

Twain, Mark. "The Mysterious Stranger." *The Project Gutenberg Book of The Mysterious Stranger and Other Stories, by Mark Twain*, 26 Aug. 2021, https://www.gutenberg.org/files/3186/3186-h/3186-h.htm#link2HCH0010.

Twenge, Jean M. *iGen: Why Today's Super-Connected Kids Are Growing Up Less Rebellious, More Tolerant, Less Happy—and Completely Unprepared for Adulthood (and What That Means for the Rest of Us)*. Atria Books, 2017.

Vogelsang, John D., and Sophia McGee. "Handbook for Facilitating Difficult Conversations in the Classroom." Teach.ufl.edu/wp-content/uploads/2016/07/Handbook-for-Facilitating-Difficult-Conversations2.Pdf, 29 July 2015.

Wharton, Edith. *The Age of Innocence*. 1920. New American Library, 1962.

"Why Facing History and Ourselves." *Facing History and Ourselves*, 2020, www.facinghistory.org/why-facing-history.

Willingham, Daniel T. "Op-Ed: Why Remote Learning Is Hard—and How to Make It Easier." *Los Angeles Times*, 18 Sept. 2020, www.latimes.com/opinion/story/2020-09-18/remote-learning-hard-make-easier.

Wilson, August. *Fences: A Play*. New American Library, 1986.

Zenger, Jack, and Joseph Folkman. "What Great Listeners Actually Do." *Harvard Business Review*, 14 July 2016, https://hbr.org/2016/07/what-great-listeners-actually-do.

Zwiers, Jeff. *Next Steps with Academic Conversations: New Ideas for Improving Learning through Classroom Talk*. Stenhouse, 2019.

Author

Susanne Rubenstein is an English teacher and writer living in Massachusetts. She is the author of three books on teaching: *Speak for Yourself: Writing with Voice; Raymond Carver in the Classroom: "A Small, Good Thing"*; and *Go Public! Encouraging Student Writers to Publish.* Her fiction and poetry have appeared in such publications as *Literal Latte, The MacGuffin,* and *The Worcester Review,* and her essays on teaching have been published in *The Christian Science Monitor, Voices from the Middle,* and *Teacher Magazine,* as well as in a number of collections. She is a Fiction Editorial Assistant for the literary journal *Carve.*

This book was typeset in TheMix and Palatino by Barbara Frazier.

Typefaces used on the cover include Populaire, Avenir Next LT Pro Medium and Medium Italic, and Just One.

The book was printed on 50-lb. White Offset paper by Sheridan.